EVALUATING THE SCHOOL LIBRARY

EVALUATING THE SCHOOL LIBRARY

ANALYSIS, TECHNIQUES, AND RESEARCH PRACTICES

SECOND EDITION

Nancy Everhart

LIBRARIES UNLIMITED®

An Imprint of ABC-CLIO, LLC

Santa Barbara, California • Denver, Colorado

Library of Congress Cataloging-in-Publication Data

Names: Everhart, Nancy, author. | Everhart, Nancy. Evaluating the school library media center.
Title: Evaluating the school library : analysis, techniques, and research practices / Nancy Everhart.
Description: Second edition. | Santa Barbara, California : Libraries Unlimited, [2021] | Includes bibliographical references and index.
Identifiers: LCCN 2020020559 (print) | LCCN 2020020560 (ebook) | ISBN 9781440855863 (paperback) | ISBN 9781440855870 (ebook)
Subjects: LCSH: School libraries—United States—Evaluation.
Classification: LCC Z675.S3 E895 2020 (print) | LCC Z675.S3 (ebook) | DDC 025.1/978—dc23
LC record available at https://lccn.loc.gov/2020020559
LC ebook record available at https://lccn.loc.gov/2020020560

ISBN: 978-1-4408-5586-3 (paperback)
        978-1-4408-5587-0 (ebook)

25 24 23 22 21   1 2 3 4 5

This book is also available as an eBook.

Libraries Unlimited
An Imprint of ABC-CLIO, LLC

ABC-CLIO, LLC
147 Castilian Drive
Santa Barbara, California 93117
www.abc-clio.com

This book is printed on acid-free paper ∞

Manufactured in the United States of America

To my grandchildren,
Jack, Kate, Max, and Helen Everhart

CONTENTS

CHAPTER 3 – COLLECTIONS

PREFACE

In today's data-driven schools, the evaluation of all programs and personnel has taken on increased importance. The terms *outcomes based*, *data for decision making*, *evidence-based practice*, *data visualization*, and *comprehensive assessment* are just a few of the phrases that can be heard traveling throughout school hallways and in faculty meetings. Many of these words were not in our school librarian vocabulary when I wrote my book *Evaluating the School Library Media Center* in 1998, over twenty years ago. But the No Child Left Behind Act in 2001 changed all that. By requiring all public schools receiving federal funding to administer a statewide standardized test annually to all students and by mandating that schools that received Title I funding make adequate yearly progress in test scores, the act put intense pressure on educators for accountability.

Although at times frustrating, the focus on evaluation can be positive for school librarians. It enables you to reflect on what is really important in your library program (students!) and to justify the decisions that you make. It encourages deep thinking. One approach to this is to keep asking yourself, "So what?" until you reach a point where you are addressing a state or national standard. If you cannot do that, you may want to reconsider the task, activity, program, service, or resource.

With the introduction of the Common Core State Standards (CCSS) in 2009, along with other state- and district-level reforms, teacher evaluation became a hot topic in many school districts across the country. Evaluation instruments for educators came under review, and this has been beneficial to school librarians, as it has provided the opportunity to develop instruments that more closely align with the numerous roles they perform. Previously, and what is still the case in many schools, school librarians' performance was assessed exclusively on the teaching role without regard to the program administrator, leader, instructional partner, and information specialist roles. Multitudes of school systems have adopted the Danielson Group's Framework for Teaching for teacher evaluation, thus stimulating state and local professional groups of school librarians to modify the instrument for use in the school library. This alignment of the evaluation of school librarians and classroom teachers can facilitate understanding of school librarians' various roles by the evaluators and also by teacher colleagues.

Facilities have changed. As new schools are built, the space for a school library has become smaller in many cases because of the dependence on electronic resources. The focus is on flexible spaces where furniture can be moved around to accommodate many needs. School libraries are incorporating makerspaces, but there has been some confusion about how to proceed, what the makerspaces should entail, and how their impact can be determined.

Do you know how to take the results from your school's standardized tests and analyze the components on literacy, problem solving, and technology learning that you have taught? Can you use data visualization (graphs, infographics) to present this data clearly to demonstrate your impact? Are rubrics being used to assess individuals? Are these rubrics valid? And finally, does the collection support the curriculum, and how do you determine this?

We are often asked whether school libraries are relevant in today's digital age. There are a variety of methods that measure digital information access and use, engagement with the library program, and use of various library areas. Instructions on how to conduct surveys and focus groups, even with very young children, are provided. Whiteboards, student response systems, and exit surveys—and their roles in encouraging student evaluations—are examined.

A new chapter on community addresses the call from professional associations for school librarians to engage with those beyond the library's four walls. Planning and evaluating this outreach are worthy tasks because of their time-consuming nature and potential to garner support for the school library program.

School libraries are certainly changing, and so the job of a school librarian is more challenging and complex. Evaluation can help. Perhaps you are a brand-new school librarian (or even an experienced one) with no idea on how your situation compares to others. Collecting data and comparing it to benchmarks will assist you in making some baseline determinations. You may want to have a neighboring school librarian, noted for having an excellent program, complete some of the surveys. Utilize that information to develop a plan to reach your goals, recognize your strengths and weaknesses, and make decisions. Once you have collected data, it is important to communicate it to the appropriate people. Share you findings with your principal, school library supervisor, students, parents, and the community. Good luck!

ACKNOWLEDGMENTS

Many thanks to Sharon Coatney, my acquisitions editor, who was very patient with me as I wrote this book. Also, a big thank-you to my graduate assistant, Zoe Hume, who is a terrific copyeditor.

I appreciate the many school librarians, library school students, and researchers who serve as inspirations as they strive to improve their programs, learn how to be leaders, and create knowledge for the field of school librarianship.

Chapter 1

General Evaluation

WHY EVALUATE?

In today's data-driven schools, the evaluation of all programs and personnel has taken on increased importance. The terms *outcomes based*, *data for decision making*, *evidence-based practice*, *data visualization*, and *comprehensive assessment* are just a few of the phrases that can be heard traveling throughout school hallways and in faculty meetings.

The school library is not exempt. As school leaders, teachers, collaborators, instructional partners, and program administrators, school librarians should be conducting evaluations as a regular, ongoing part of the program. There are several reasons for performing evaluations. First, you want to know whether you are in sync with your school's mission. Are you responsive to student, faculty, and administrative concerns and objectives? Schools are constantly changing organisms: curricula change, faculty change, and county, state, and national initiatives change. What worked in the past in your library may not be working now, and you need to administer an evaluation to find out why. Perhaps you have introduced a new reading program, instructional method, or technology, or maybe you moved or bought new furniture. Your collection may have been moved, weeded, or rearranged by genre. The entire scope of your program may have been transformed from a traditional library into a learning commons or a digital library that is more often accessed from classrooms and homes rather than in person.

Evaluations conducted before and after any changes have occurred will be useful in determining their impact.

Collecting hard data on various aspects of your library program lends credence when you must communicate program needs to administrators. You make a better impression when you come into a meeting with concrete numbers and maybe even charts, graphs, or infographics to get your point across. Data is a necessity when applying for grant funding. You need to prove to the agency providing the funds, in definitive terms, why the money is needed and what is to be accomplished with it.

Perhaps you are a brand-new school librarian (or even an experienced one) with no idea how your situation compares to others. The tools and data presented here will assist you in making some baseline determinations. You may want to have a neighboring school librarian, noted for having an excellent program, complete some of the surveys. Utilize that information to develop a plan to reach your goals, recognize your strengths and weaknesses, and make decisions. On a broader scale, evaluations may be required by administrators who wish to compare their programs at the local level or to gain accreditation by state or regional agencies, such as the Texas Private School Accreditation Commission or the North Central Association of Colleges and Schools.

BEFORE YOU START

Larger school districts, particularly those near universities, have review boards that have established guidelines for research. The board approves studies before they can move forward, ensuring that students and staff will be protected. Although the activities in this book are not the traditional formal type of research study, it would be best to check with the board, if there is one in your district, before administering surveys or conducting interviews. The board will require that participants remain anonymous, which is a compulsory procedure for anyone conducting surveys and is also helpful in obtaining objective, honest responses. If there is no such governing body where you work, checking with the principal is good practice.

TYPES OF EVALUATION

School library evaluation is either quantitative or qualitative. Quantitative evaluation involves collecting numerical information, such as number of checkouts, collection and equipment counts, hits to the library's website, number of classes using the library, number of lessons planned with teachers, or size of budget. Quantitative evaluation is a good place to start, especially for a novice school librarian. Many of the studies and guidelines in this book suggest types of quantitative data to collect to be used for comparison purposes.

Table 1-1   Qualitative and Quantitative Measures

Quantitative Measures	Qualitative Measures
Number of lessons planned with teachers	Level of planning
Circulation of fiction books	Students' success rate in finding a desired fiction book
Number of periodical databases	Percentage of citations from databases in student research papers
Library attendance	Students' satisfaction with library hours

However, there is some danger in relying solely on quantitative evaluation. According to Woolls, "Administrators could place too much emphasis on counting things with little regard for their quality. Collections may meet an arbitrary numerical count but be out of date, in poor condition, or of no value to the current curriculum" (2008, 204–205). Circulation and visit counts mean virtually nothing when a school is on a fixed schedule and every student takes out two books per week.

Quality is harder to gauge but ultimately more important. Qualitative measures often involve surveying or interviewing users about their satisfaction with the services, collections, and facilities of the library or calculating how information needs are met. Table 1.1 helps to clarify the distinctions between quantitative and qualitative measures.

Library evaluation makes an attempt to characterize the goodness of a library. In other words, we may ask, "How good is a library?" (quality) or "What does a good library do?" (value) (Orr 1973). A school library may contain a substantial collection of fiction books, but if they are all in English, they are of no value to a predominantly Spanish-speaking population.

INPUTS, OUTPUTS, AND OUTCOMES

Keeping track of tangible assets such as collections, equipment, and furniture (inputs) is a task traditionally performed by many school librarians. Compiling circulation and attendance statistics (outputs) is also a rote activity, without much thought going into how to use these statistics for comparisons, trend analysis, and achievement of goals. But these and other inputs and outputs can be collected, put to use in simple formulas, and interpreted for beneficial school library evaluation and even for making a case for more staff, higher budgets, and schedule changes (Bradburn 1999). The chapter on collections provides examples.

"Outcomes are an entirely different matter. They are changes experienced by library users—changes in knowledge, skills, attitude, behavior, status, or condition. So, some might find it helpful to substitute for the sound-alike terms *input*, *output*, and *outcome* 'library resources,' 'library services,' and 'user changes'" (Lyons and Lance 2014). Gross, Mediavilla, and Walter (2016) maintain that input and output measures do not tell us how library programs benefit participants; outcomes focus on human impact, which is often described through the participants' own words. Outcomes are used in the chapters on students, curriculum, and facilities.

Logic Models

In evaluation, the logic model is used to help structure indicators around a framework that reflects a certain linear way of thinking about a program. Indicators are developed for inputs and activities to measure what resources are being used and what they are being used for; outputs to see how much the inputs and activities are being used by the target audience; and outcomes to measure how much change is occurring in people or communities as a result of the outputs (Becker 2015). For example, many school libraries display student artwork. But really think about the reasons you do this in terms of outputs:

We display student artwork in the library

so that

Students feel a sense of belonging in their library

so that

They will come to the library more often

so that

They will discover and use our resources

so that

They will support their learning

so that

They raise their achievement.

EVALUATION METHODS

The various types of evaluation methods used in libraries can be categorized as questionnaires, interviews, numbers gathering, and observation. These methods are complementary and can be used in combination to evaluate a service or project. Each of these techniques is discussed here within the context of the school library.

Questionnaires

Questionnaires, or surveys, can be used to gather information that is self-reported, reported from others, or reported from records. Throughout this book, there are numerous questionnaires. Many of these are to gather self-reported information such as the types of services offered, equipment, physical resources, and curriculum involvement. Because most school libraries are one-person operations, you are in a knowledgeable position to answer these questions. An example of a self-reported survey in this book is a knowledge of your community survey. The advantage of self-reported information is that it can be gathered very quickly. The information can be put to use in a planning process in a short amount of time. Usually outside agencies, such as accrediting organizations, require a "self-study" to get you started in thinking about future goals and objectives.

Other questionnaires in this book involve asking others—students, faculty, administration, and parents—for their input. Survey responses from others are especially useful for measuring attitudes. Surveys allow you to gather data from a large number of people in a short time, and the data can be easily analyzed and summarized. Today, there are a variety of tools that are helpful in producing surveys. If you want to construct a paper survey, you can use any word processing program. Microsoft Office has survey templates in Word (or you can create your own), and an array of templates can be found by searching Google Images for *survey template* or using Google Forms. Pinterest (www.pinterest.com) and Teachers Pay Teachers (www .teacherspayteachers.com) are other sources. You may want to conduct an online survey using the numerous tools that are free or moderately priced and work quite well (Schindler and Rubin 2018). All of them guide you step by step through creating a survey, sharing the survey, and evaluating the results. Your school district may already have survey software included in its management system that would be available for school librarians to use.

Examples of questionnaires asking others for input are in the chapters on students and curriculum.

If you are interested in composing your own surveys, the following tips will aid in improving their quality:

- Avoid questions that ask respondents to rank items (e.g., "rank the importance of the following library services to you from most to least important"). Not only are rankings hard to analyze, but they are also misleading as it's possible that all of the items asked about could be of equal importance to respondents. A better approach is to ask respondents to rate items (e.g., "rate the importance of each of the following library services to you on a scale where 5=extremely important and 1=not at all important").
- Include some open-ended questions.
- Do not use lines with open-ended questions. Instead, leave that area as white space.
- Do not "break" your questions or carry them from one page to another.
- Include page numbers.

- Include a closing statement. In addition to thanking patrons for participating in the survey, this statement might also include contact information should respondents have any questions about the survey.
- After drafting your library's survey, have colleagues proofread it for clarity and to assess the validity of the questions included.
- Use short questions when possible.
- Carefully consider the placement of each question and set of related questions.
- Number the items consecutively from the beginning to the end.
- Use plenty of white space to ensure that the survey is readable.
- Use an easy-to-read font size and type.
- Use lead-ins for new or lengthy sections to orient and guide the user. For example, if your survey includes a demographics section, title it as such.
- Provide clear instructions.
- Avoid multiple-response questions.
- Refrain from using "double-barreled" questions. These are questions that combine 2 or more topics, such that the researcher cannot know which "barrel" of the question was answered. An example would be, "Do you think that the library is important and would you support a mill levy for increased funding?" If the words "and" or "or" are included in your question, it might be double-barreled. (Library Research Service 2018)

It is good practice to have a small group of people take the survey to clarify any misunderstandings and to determine whether you are getting back the type of data that you want before launching a large-scale survey. Piloting the survey provides the opportunity to make any edits before launching a large-scale survey.

Questionnaires employ measurement scales. The various types are shown here with examples:

Yes or No answer:
I visit the library during lunch periods. _____ yes _____ no

Checklist:
Check the statement that best represents how easy it is to use the library's website:
_____ Able to use without help
_____ Able to use with onscreen help
_____ Able to use with the librarian's help
_____ Able to use with another student's help
_____ Not able to use

Scaled responses:

How often were books you needed for school assignments not available for the following reasons:

	(4) Often	(3) Sometimes	(2) Rarely	(1) Never
Checked out	_____	_____	_____	_____
Missing from shelves	_____	_____	_____	_____
Lost	_____	_____	_____	_____
Mutilated (pages missing)	_____	_____	_____	_____

Please circle the number that corresponds to how satisfied you are with the following in the library:

	No Opinion	Very Dissatisfied	Somewhat Dissatisfied	Somewhat Satisfied	Very Satisfied
Seating	1	2	3	4	5
Lighting	1	2	3	4	5
Heat/air conditioning	1	2	3	4	5
Signs	1	2	3	4	5
Noise level	1	2	3	4	5
Cleanliness	1	2	3	4	5
Furnishings	1	2	3	4	5

How do you rate the library staff?

Discourteous	1----------2----------3----------4----------5	Courteous
Not Helpful	1----------2----------3----------4----------5	Helpful

Three-point scales:

Low	Moderate	High
Higher	Same	Lower
Greater	Equal	Less
Definitely agree	Neutral	Definitely disagree
Above average	Average	Below average
Very often	Occasionally	Never

Four-point scales:

Many	Some	Very few	None
Excellent	Good	Fair	Poor
Daily	Weekly	Occasionally	Never
Daily	Weekly	Monthly	Once a semester

Five-point scales:

Strongly approve	Approve	Undecided	Disapprove	Strongly disapprove
Very high	Above average	Average	Below average	Very low
Strongly Agree	Agree	Neutral	Disagree	Strongly disagree
Poor	Below average	Above average	Average	Excellent
Always	Usually	Sometimes	Rarely	Never
Very poor	Poor	Fair	Good	Very good
Excellent	Very good	Average	Fair	Poor

Ranking in order of importance:

Please rank (1 to 5, with 5 being most important) what you do to get magazine articles not available in our school library:

____ Requested through interlibrary loan
____ Went to local university library
____ Went to local public library
____ Didn't try to get article
____ Used the abstract of the article

Graphic surveys:

For younger children and those who may have lower-level reading skills, pictures or emojis can be used instead of text (see figure 1.1).

Students can participate in polling using personal response systems, also known as clickers. Tablets, mobile phones, and laptops can also be used as a response system to answer multiple-choice questions that have been projected. The devices can interface with an interactive whiteboard to display totaled responses.

Open-ended questions:

1. Are there any materials, equipment, or services that you think the library should offer that it does not currently?
2. What do you enjoy doing most in the library?
3. What aspect of the library most needs improvement?

Even if a survey is predominantly multiple-choice or scaled responses, you should ask an open-ended question at the end, such as, "Is there anything you would like to add?" or "What else should we know?" to capture as much information as possible.

Interviews

"Interviewing is necessary when we cannot observe behavior, feelings, or how people interpret the world around them" (Merriam and Tisdell 2016).

6. How do you feel about starting a new book?

7. How do you feel about reading during summer vacation?

Figure 1.1 Sample questions from the Elementary Reading Attitude Survey
Source: Adapted from McKenna and Kear 1990.

Interviews may be especially useful in gaining input from elementary schoolchildren, as the chief skill needed by the respondent is the ability to speak. Interviewing children requires the interviewer to flexibly adapt their methods to match children's developing cognitive, linguistic, social, and psychological competencies. Gibson (2012) provides guidance for interviews and focus groups with young children:

Building Trust

- Be familiar with and to the children before starting the interview.
- Have teachers present at the first meeting.
- Opt for a friendly and relaxed manner.
- Form a partnership with the children, not a hierarchical relationship.

Facilitating understanding and obtaining informed consent:

- Use child-friendly language to convey the purpose of the study.
- Inform children you are interested in their thoughts and feelings.
- Use ground rules to clarify the role that children will play in the interview process:
    - You can say "pass" if you do not want to answer.
    - Take time to think before you answer.
    - Tell me if I do not understand you or if you do not understand me.
    - There are no right or wrong answers; say what you want.
    - I will not tell other people what you say.
    - Take turns talking.
    - No teasing or making fun.

- Invite questions and provide clarification.
- Obtain consent only after children fully understand the study and their role.

Encouraging thoughtful and detailed responses:

- Start with questions that can be answered with a brief, easy response.
- Primarily use open-ended questions.
- Encourage detail by using follow-up questions and prompts.
- Be patient; do not be too quick to redirect or jump to conclusions.
- Refrain from providing cues or assistance in answering a question.
- Use reflective statements, summary statements, acknowledgment of feelings, and generous praise for engagement.
- Sit squared off in an open and relaxed manner; maintain eye contact; and match the child's level of movement.

Promoting enjoyment and creative expression:

- Allow for movement or engage in a familiar task, such as walking, drawing, or playing a nonverbal game.
- Use drawing, journaling, role-play, and props.

There are different types of questions that are typically asked in interviews. These will vary depending on the information that is being solicited. Among these are the following:

- *Experience and behavior questions* probe what a person does or has done, with the intent of eliciting descriptions of behaviors, actions, and activities that are observable. "Why did you start your search with those terms?"
- *Feeling questions* seek to elicit the emotional responses of people based on their experiences and thoughts. The questioner is looking for adjectives that describe feelings, such as *happy*, *frustrated*, *upset*, and *anxious*. "What makes you feel creative when you are in the library?"
- *Opinion and value questions* are aimed at understanding the thought processes of the respondent. The questioner is seeking information pertaining to goals, desires, values, and intentions. "How might you use what you learned today to help you with assignments in the future?"
- *Knowledge questions* are asked to determine the level of knowledge and information the respondent has about a particular topic. "How do you find images for your presentation?"

- *Sensory questions* ask about what is seen, heard, touched, tasted, and smelled. "When you walk into the library, what do you see?"
- *Demographic questions* identify the characteristics of the respondent. "How long have you been at our school?" (Matthews 2015)

Focus Groups

A popular interview method for evaluation is the focus group interview. A focus group consists of a small representative sampling of those people whose opinions you are interested in obtaining. They are interviewed together because group dynamics make it easier for some people to express attitudes, ideas, and opinions. When interviewing children, it is better if the participants do not know each other well. For example, you could choose about seven or eight freshmen to interview about how your orientation program for new students could be improved, or a teacher from each grade in an elementary school could be chosen to provide feedback as to library's physical layout. You may want to combine a focus group interview before a written survey for some ideas as to the types of questions to ask or after a survey has been analyzed to clarify certain responses.

Focus group interviews usually last about thirty to forty-five minutes with children and from forty-five to ninety minutes with adults. You will usually ask about five open-ended questions with possible follow-ups for clarification (Cook and Farmer 2011). This sample set of questions was designed to find out how middle school students use the library's video production studio:

1. What do you use the video studio for?
2. When do you use it?
3. What do you think about it?
4. How do you think improvements could be made in regard to our video studio?
5. What is the best thing about the video studio?

When conducting a focus group interview with young people, here are some suggestions:

- Have the meeting in a comfortable, safe, and neutral location. Most participants like to sit around a table, but sometimes children feel more at ease on pillows on the floor.
- Have a tape recorder (with good batteries) and audiocassette plainly visible on the table.

- Explain again what you are doing and why. Be brief.
- Assure participants that what they say is confidential, that the tape will only be used to help you remember what was said, and that no one will be identified in any written report of the focus group. Tell them what will be done with their input; for example, it will be included in a report that goes to the school board. (Avoid promising any action as a result of their input.) Be brief.
- Explain that this is not a test; there are no right and wrong answers. Be clear that you genuinely want to know what they think. Again, be brief. You want to listen to them.
- Keep note taking to a minimum. Concentrate your attention on listening and understanding what you are hearing. It is helpful to have a colleague present to listen and take notes.
- Encourage each person to respond to each other's questions, but respect any person's desire to remain silent.
- Allow participants to respond to each other; sometimes you get the best insights from their interaction.
- Keep participants on the topic unless their digressions are potentially useful.
- Avoid giving your own opinions or judgments on what is said. Active listening techniques may encourage and clarify the discussion, however. Try occasionally repeating a participant's statement in slightly different words.
- When you have finished your prepared questions, ask whether there are any last remarks that will help you understand what the participants have to say on this subject.
- Thank everyone for participating. Assure the participants that they have been helpful.
- Avoid promising the participants that they will see the results of the focus group unless you have already agreed to this as a condition of their participation. (Walter 1992)

To analyze the results of the focus group interview, listen to the tape again as soon as possible and make note of major themes, issues, and concerns. Write down three or four major themes. These are your findings. Support each statement with several direct quotes from the taped discussion; this is your evidence (Walter 1992). Let's look at the example of students' use of the video production studio.

A. Students use the video production studio for class projects.
  - "In history, I made a video from the perspective of a historical figure."
  - "We're required to do a group video project for Spanish class in which we only speak Spanish."

B. Students use the video production studio for personal needs.
- "The green screen is awesome! I love to make videos with all types of cool backgrounds."
- "We recorded our poetry slam."
- "Jason made a great highlight reel of our soccer season. It had music and special effects too."

C. Students find it frustrating when they do not have access to equipment.
- "Three times straight, when our science class came to the library to work on our project, I didn't have time to use the shared equipment."
- "I think we should be able to use our cell phone cameras in the studio because there aren't enough cameras."

From your results, you can write a report using the following outline:

1. Purpose of the study.
2. Study procedures. Describe focus groups (and any other methods used to collect data).
3. Results. Use the format described in the previous section.
4. Discussion. Elaborate on the implications of the results.
5. Recommendations. (Walter 1992)

In this instance, you may want to use the results of your focus group interviews to make recommendations to purchase more cameras or to advocate for a policy change that would allow cell phones to be used for educational purposes in the school.

Alternate Interview Methods

There are techniques that go beyond the traditional practice of question and answer that have been well established in the field of childhood studies. Toys and models facilitate children's accounts of personally experienced events (Priestley and Pipe 1997). In one example, researchers were able to encourage young children to participate in a focus group interview by initially telling a story about a bear who loves books and loves to read (Jug and Vilar 2015). The combination of the story and interview maintained the children's attention, offered them further explanation of the questions they had to answer, and maintained the focus of the interview. While the moderator was telling a story to the children, she animated them with a plush teddy bear to which they were actually answering, not paying any attention to the moderator herself.

Interviewing young children presents a challenge because they tend to provide incomplete accounts and are easily misled. Therefore, there is a need for techniques to improve young children's recall while maintaining accuracy and increasing completeness. Computer-assisted interviews offer a way for young children to provide accounts of their experiences and have yielded high-quality responses (Fängström et al. 2016).

James (2001) describes a variety of task-centered activities as approaches to collect data in individual and focus group interviews that "encourage children to engage in some type of activity that allows them to communicate their ideas, opinions, and perspectives by other than solely verbal means" (quoted in Barriage 2018). These activities include drawings, photography, drama, play and games, child-led tours, diaries, and participatory activities such as concept mapping, card sorting, and collaborative storytelling (Johnson, Hart, and Colwell 2014).

Observation

Observation is a method for learning about the activities of a library customer. By simple observation, you can gain an understanding of the successes and challenges of your users. Observing student interactions and areas of high and low use in the library can yield valuable information that illuminates what is found in surveys or interviews. Observing peers and other school libraries aids in evaluating your own by way of comparison. Principals evaluate their librarians almost solely based on observation (Everhart 2006).

When using observation as an evaluation technique, one needs to define the behavior to be studied and standardize the process used to observe. According to Johnson (1996), you need to determine the following:

1. What you are trying to learn. What will you study, and why is it important? Sharply defining what will be studied and how results will be used will increase chances of collecting interpretable and useful data.
2. Where you are going to make the observations. Observations could be of one grade level, all computer stations, or other defined locations. Explicitly defining the locations at which to make observations helps in knowing where results could be applied.
3. When the observations will occur. Library use differs by time of day, day of the week, time of year, and so on. The main concern with sampling is representativeness: are the times selected for study representative of the overall use of the library in the aspect being studied?
4. Who will make the observations? In a school library, this will most likely be the school librarian. It is important to not attract notice that you recording your observations so as not to alter the behavior of the people being observed.

5. How the observations will be made. Make test observations to determine how observations will be made and to learn how well procedures work. The resulting methods should be included in the report of the results of the observation.

6. How the observations will be recorded. Comparability of observations requires that they are recorded in a standardized form. Evaluation designers should create and test a form that will include the needed information, such as who made the observation, when it occurred, where it occurred, and what was observed.

7. How the results will be analyzed. A plan for analyzing the results should be in place before data collection has begun. How to analyze the data will be guided by thinking about the kinds of statements you intend to make in the conclusions. For example, if you want to be able to discuss how long users wait to use the stations, then the observation form must have a place for noting the times a given user arrives in line and starts using the station. The analysis will involve making a calculation of the time spent by subtracting the time of arrival from the time of sitting down. The report will need to summarize the observed times so that an administrator can see their range and pattern. If you want to make a statement such as "Half of our users spend more than ___ minutes waiting to take tests for our reading program," to justify purchasing more stations, your results will have to be arranged in order of time spent waiting so that it is possible to identify the middle score (the median).

8. How to report the results. From the beginning, it is well to think about the report of findings. In general, the task of the report is to explain the data presented and to interpret it in terms of the reasons for the study. (Return to point 1: What you are trying to learn.) To communicate the richness of the observations made, it is likely that the report will contain a mix of numerical data and narrative description: "Students checked out all the books available by the visiting author, and over two-thirds have waiting lists of at least ten." One student called out to her friends, "I'm going to ask my mom to buy this book!"

Observation techniques are used in the chapters on facilities and personnel.

Using Existing Data

Observation, interviews, and surveys are data collection methods that can be time-consuming and potentially intrusive. But there are ready-made sources of data easily accessible to school librarians. These types of data sources can exist in both a physical setting and an online setting as shown in tables 1.2 and 1.3 (Merriam and Tisdell 2016).

Existing data are used in the chapters on personnel and community.

Table 1-2   Sample Composite Survey Data in Self-Study on Information Resources for Middle States Accreditation

Information Resources	Parents	Students	Staff
12.1 The school provides students with adequate library/media resources and services. Information resources are properly catalogued, housed, and periodically reviewed for relevancy and currency.	3.34	3.35	3.29
12.2 The media center staff is sufficient and appropriately qualified to provide effective series to students and staff.	N/A	N/A	3.25
12.3 Adequate orientation about the use of media services, learning resources, and equipment is provided to the staff and students.	N/A	3.14	3.20
12.4 Information resources are appropriately supported annually with funding from the school's budget.	N/A	N/A	3.21
12.5 Information resources are age and developmentally appropriate, current, and reflect social and cultural diversity.	2.78	3.01	3.27
12.6 Staff and students are provided opportunities to offer input into the types, quality, and format of the information resources provided.	N/A	2.35	3.13

Rating of Adherence to the Indicator

1. Does not meet	The evidence indicates the school **does not meet** the expectations of this indicator.
2. Partially meets/in need of improvement	The evidence indicates the school **partially meets** the expectations of this indicator and is **in need of improvement**.
3. Meets	The evidence indicates the school **meets** the expectations of this indicator.
4. Exceeds	The evidence indicates the school **exceeds** the expectations of this indicator.

Table 1-3   Some Sources of Existing Data Related to the School Library

Physical	Online
Photos of the library in yearbooks	Social media discussions
Student standardized test scores in reading	Circulation reports
Student projects, bibliographies	Transaction logs
In-house use	Survey statistics for benchmarking

GETTING STARTED

Conducting an overall self-evaluation of all the components of your school library media program is an efficient way to identify areas that need improvement or further investigation. A good tool is provided by the South Dakota State Library (figure 1.2). Other self-assessments are available through the

21st Century | 2018
School Library | through
Self-Assessment | 2021

21st Century school libraries and librarians make a powerful difference in student achievement and are partners in forming the habit of reading and learning for a lifetime.

South Dakota School Library Mission Statement

It is the mission of the school library to:

1. Provide all learners a 21st Century collaborative program for learning and teaching;
2. Provide a place for both a physical and a virtual learning environment; and
3. Provide access to a highly qualified professional for leadership in creating, promoting, and sustaining the program and place

Self-Assessment Information

The South Dakota School Library Guidelines* outline the best practices of a **21st Century school library**. We encourage librarians and administrators to use this voluntary self-assessment tool as an aid in implementing the guidelines. This tool can be a catalyst for conversations concerning future planning and development. It can serve as a checklist toward strategic planning and annual goals. It can also supplement the work of the library and librarian when used in conjunction with the School Library Collection Development Plan Framework and Student Assessment in the School Library Framework.

The South Dakota State Library, a division of the Department of Education, formally and annually recognizes schools with libraries that meet the characteristics of a 21st Century school library through its program, place, and professional. Awards recognize the status of the library as *Effective (75-79), Enhanced (80-83), or Exemplary (84-87)* based on the South Dakota School Library Guidelines. If the overall score of your 21st Century School Library Self-Assessment falls within one of the three point ranges noted above, you are eligible to apply for the 21st Century School Library Award. You can also use the self-assessment tool as a worksheet to complete the award application. Applications are accepted **March 1 through May 1** of each year. Award status is valid for a three-year period.

For further inquiries and technical assistance, please contact Alissa Adams by email: alissa.adams@state.sd.us or by phone: 605.295.3152

*South Dakota School Library Guidelines: http://www.library.sd.gov/LIB/SLC/index.aspx#Guideline
Adopted by the South Dakota Board of Education, July 2012
Adopted by the South Dakota State Library Board, June 2012
Endorsed by the South Dakota Library Association, July 2012

Apply Online Today!

Figure 1.2   Twenty-First-Century School Library Self-Assessment

Source: South Dakota State Library.

Please use the following scale to rate your library on the items below:

3 = consistently exemplifies highest quality performance
2 = generally meets requirements in most areas
1 = striving to improve in areas known to be deficient
0 = falls short of meeting guidelines or hindered by barriers

THE THREE E'S: Effective, Enhanced, Exemplary				
PLACE: Learning Environment	3	2	1	0
Space: Accommodates a variety of activities: individual, small groups, large groups, special events, professional development Examples include, but are not limited to: • *areas for instruction and reading* • *seating for more than one class* • *large presentation area and/or dedicated adjoining small room/s* • *computer access area*				
Access: Provides flexible and equitable access during school day, before and after school Examples include, but are not limited to: • *schedule allows access for students from all grade levels during school day* • *schedule allows for before and after school access for all students* • *combination of fixed and flexible schedule allows for class access at point of need* • *schedule allows for special group meetings*				
Technology: Provides access to a variety of current technology for learners Examples include, but are not limited to: • *desktop computers and/or laptops, wifi access, outlets* • *audio and video production tools* • *tablets, ereaders, and MP3 players* • *interactive whiteboard, document camera, digital projection*				
Atmosphere: Holds inviting, secure, age-appropriate furnishings and storage Examples include, but are not limited to: • *student friendly and safe; library "belongs to all" attitude* • *displays, lighting, signage as needed* • *flexible shelving and furniture sized for age of students and accessible to all* • *learning hub for all content areas*				
Resource Collection: Meets needs of population and curriculum through physical and virtual collection Examples include, but are not limited to: • *adequate and continually updated print and digital collections* • *collections reflect school population size, academic and personal interests of students* • *24/7 access to digital resources* • *web-based online catalog access*				
Budget: Supports mission, stability, and growth through an annual budget Examples include, but are not limited to: • *dedicated district funding for resources and technology* • *budget requests based on needs assessment* • *inclusion in Title and/or grant proposals*				
Staff: Contains trained staff to instruct, guide, and support learners – both students and staff Examples include, but are not limited to: • *librarian or support staff available during all open hours* • *staff trained in reader's advisory, research, technology tools, curriculum* • *staff guide and supervise adult and/or student volunteers*				
TOTAL: Place				

Figure 1.2   Continued

PROFESSIONAL: Leadership for Learning	3	2	1	0
Teaching Staff: Is a certified teacher librarian employed by the school Examples include, but are not limited to: • *certified teacher with MLIS* • *certified teacher with library endorsement* • *full-time or part-time as usage and school population dictate*				
Support Staff: Supervises a paid staff assistant Examples include, but are not limited to: • *paraprofessional in addition to certified staff* • *full-time or part-time as usage and school population dictate* • *adult and/or student volunteers supplement work of employed staff*				
Online Presence: Maintains an online library presence Examples include, but are not limited to: • *promotes a web-based catalog* • *maintains a library website, wiki, blog, etc.* • *maintains a library presence on social media sites*				
Leadership: Participates in building, district, state, and/or national curriculum and/or as a planning committee member Examples include, but are not limited to: • *serves on curriculum/standards committees* • *serves on building/district technology committees* • *serves on building/district school improvement committees* • *communicates with administrators and other stakeholders regarding the library*				
Professional Organizations: Participates as a member of library-related professional organization(s) Examples include, but are not limited to: • *South Dakota examples: SDLA, SDEA, SDRC* • *Regional examples: MPLA* • *National examples: ALA, AASL, ISTE, ASCD*				
Professional Development: Participates in and presents professional development Examples include, but are not limited to: • *develops a personal learning network* • *attends and presents at school and/or district in-services* • *attends online classes and/or webinars for CEU or renewal credit* • *attends professional conferences/presents at conferences and/or webinars*				
Teaching Practices: Implements best teaching practices based on current data and trends Examples include, but are not limited to: • *integrates Common Core Standards with State Library Standards* • *adheres to concepts of Danielson Framework for Teaching* • *applies new and emerging technology to learning and teaching* • *co-teaches and assesses inquiry-based and collaborative group projects*				
Collaboration: Collaborates to co-teach with other staff members Examples include, but are not limited to: • *attends collaboration meetings to plan for co-teaching units/lessons* • *regularly communicates, cooperates and collaborates with staff in person and using digital tools* • *assumes leadership role in promoting integration across all content areas*				
Ethical Model: Models ethical participation in global world Examples include, but are not limited to: • *models safe and appropriate digital footprint* • *models knowledge of fair use and copyright* • *models responsible behavior when communicating in all formats*				

Figure 1.2 Continued

Professional: Leadership for Learning (Continued)	3	2	1	0
Policies and Procedures: Creates, maintains, and updates board-approved library policies and procedures Examples include, but are not limited to: • *creates a collection development policy, including a weeding and donations policy and a reconsideration policy and procedure* • *develops a circulation policy and related procedures* • *collaborates to develop a responsible use policy for students and staff* • *policies and procedures are reviewed and approved by library advisory board and school board on a regular basis*				
Management: Uses current techniques and technology to manage library procedures and collection Examples include, but are not limited to: • *maintains an integrated library system(ILS): circulation, cataloging, ordering, OPAC* • *utilizes ILS reports for collection development and other statistical reports* • *applies creativity, flexibility and best practices in field of librarianship*				
Strategic Plan: Develops library strategic plan with school- and/or community-based advisory group Examples include, but are not limited to: • *develops mission that is aligned with school and district* • *conducts a needs assessment on a regular basis* • *develops goals and objectives on a regular basis* • *collects qualitative and quantitative data to annually assess strategic plan*				
Reading Model: Models and encourages a love of reading Examples include, but are not limited to: • *promotes new resources through print and digital tools* • *provides book talks in the library and/or classrooms* • *promotes and models reading for personal enjoyment and meeting personal information needs*				
TOTAL: Professional				

PROGRAM: Learning and Teaching	3	2	1	0
Mission: Upholds a board-adopted library mission statement with goals and objectives, aligned with overall mission of school and district Examples include, but are not limited to: • *available to the public, posted in library, website, etc.* • *reviewed and aligned annually by library advisory and school boards* • *directs daily collection development, instruction, events, activities*				
Collaboration: Supports collaboration across content areas with resources, planning, and co-teaching Examples include, but are not limited to: • *integrates school-wide initiatives such as character education, anti-bullying, etc.* • *provides collaborative tools and guides for students and staff such as website, wikis, emails, pathfinders, etc.* • *provides resources to support instruction*				
Reading Promotion: Promotes reading for academic and personal learning for all levels and abilities Examples include, but are not limited to: • *hosts book fairs and family literacy events* • *promotes state and national book award programs* • *promotes resources through reader's advisory, class instruction, digital tools* • *coordinates book clubs and library/school/community events*				
Resource Collection: Maintains a current and balanced collection of physical and digital resources Examples include, but are not limited to: • *maintains and updates multicultural collection of resources in all formats* • *maintains and updates resources at all levels of abilities as needed and in all formats* • *maintains and updates resources in all genres and to support all content areas*				

Figure 1.2 Continued

20

Program: Learning and Teaching (Continued)	3	2	1	0
Multiple Literacies: Promotes and provides for instruction in multiple literacies Examples include, but are not limited to: • *provides opportunities to read, view and listen in all formats* • *co-teaches to integrate new and emerging digital tools and resources* • *provides instruction in information, visual, media, and technology literacies* • *implements information search process model across all grade levels*				
Special Events and Programs: Promotes and sponsors special events and programs school- and community-wide Examples include, but are not limited to: • *cooperates and collaborates with public library for summer reading programs, featured authors/speakers, teen advisory boards, etc.* • *promotes state and national school library initiatives* • *develops partnerships in local community*				
Learner Assessments: Includes the creation and completion of informal and formal assessments Examples include, but are not limited to: • *develops formative assessments for daily instruction* • *develops rubrics, checklists, electronic portfolios and other summative assessments in conjunction with content teachers* • *uses a variety of diagnostic tools to assess student learning in multiple literacies*				
Technology Tools: Utilizes computer, Internet, and video/audio technology as tools for learning and teaching Examples include, but are not limited to: • *provides instruction utilizing technology tools for research, evaluation and production* • *provides instruction for outside-of-school access to resources* • *provides instruction that leads to college and career readiness and lifelong learning habits*				
Standards Alignment: Aligns instruction and resources with local curriculum, state content standards, and national initiatives Examples include, but are not limited to: • *resources are mapped to support curriculum of all content areas* • *lesson plans link to library and Common Core standards and are available to stakeholders* • *provides a scaffolded approach to inquiry*				
TOTAL: Program				
TOTAL: Place, Professional, and Program				

21st Century School Library Self-Assessment Total Point Ranges:
Effective: 75-79   Enhanced: 80-83   Exemplary: 84-87

Apply Online Today!

Figure 1.2   Continued

State of Florida Department of Education (n.d.) and New York State Education Department (2016).

The South Dakota form contains sections for Program (Learning and Teaching), Place (Learning Environment), and Professional (Leadership for Learning). Each of these sections provides concrete examples for measuring engagement in subcategories from 0–3. Scores add up to a potential 100, with 75–79 scoring Effective, 80–83 scoring Enhanced, and 84–87 scoring Exemplary. This form is good for illustrating what these behaviors look like. New York's rubric provides excellent examples but also enables self-assessment using the categories of Distinguished, Proficient, Basic, and Below Basic in Essential Elements of the program. The detail in each cell of the rubric is outstanding because the form is also designed to be used by administrators and parents.

REFERENCES

Barriage, Sarah. 2018. "Task-Centered Activities as an Approach to Data Collection in Research with Children and Youth." *Library & Information Science Research* 40 (1): 1–8. doi:10.1016/j.lisr.2018.01.001.

Becker, Samantha. 2015. "Outcomes, Impacts, and Indicators." *Library Journal*, September 18. https://www.libraryjournal.com/?detailStory =outcomes-impacts-and-indicators.

Bradburn, Frances Bryant. 1999. *Output Measures for School Library Media Programs*. New York: Neal-Schuman Publishers.

Cook, Douglas, and Lesley S. J. Farmer. 2011. *Using Qualitative Methods in Action Research: How Librarians Can Get to the Why of Data*. Chicago: Association of College and Research Libraries.

Everhart, Nancy. 2006. "Principals' Evaluation of School Librarians: A Study of Strategic and Nonstrategic Evidence-Based Approaches." *School Libraries Worldwide* 12 (2): 38–51. https://iasl-online.org /Resources/Documents/slw/v12/12_2everhart.pdf.

Fängström, Karin, Pär Bokström, Anton Dahlberg, Rachel Calam, Steven Lucas, and Anna Sarkadi. 2016. "In My Shoes—Validation of a Computer Assisted Approach for Interviewing Children." *Child Abuse & Neglect* 58: 160–72. doi:10.1016/j.chiabu.2016.06.022.

Florida Department of Education. Library Media Services. n.d. "ExC3EL— Florida's K-12 Library Program Evaluation Tool." http://www.fldoe.org

/academics/standards/subject-areas/library-media-services-instructional
-t/exc3el-fls-k-12-library-program-evalua.stml.

Gibson, Jennifer E. 2012. "Interviews and Focus Groups with Children: Methods That Match Children's Developing Competencies." *Journal of Family Theory & Review* 4 (2): 148–59. doi:10.1111/j.1756-2589.2012.00119.x.

Gross, Melissa, Cindy Mediavilla, and Virginia A. Walter. 2016. *Five Steps of Out-Based Planning and Evaluation for Public Libraries*. Chicago: ALA Editions.

James, Allison. 2001. "Ethnography in the Study of Children and Childhood." In *Handbook of Ethnography*, edited by Paul Atkinson, Amanda Coffey, Sara Delamont, John Lofland, and Lyn Lofland, 246–57. Thousand Oaks, CA: SAGE.

Johnson, Debra Wilcox. 1996. "Evaluation Methods." In *The Tell It! Manual: The Complete Program for Evaluating Library Performance*, edited by Douglas Zweizig, Debra Wilcox Johnson, Jane Robbins, and Michele Besand, 113–20. Chicago and London: American Library Association.

Johnson, Vicky, Roger Hart, and Jennifer Colwell, eds. 2014. *Steps to Engaging Young People in Research*. 2 vols. The Hague: Bernard van Leer Foundation.

Jug, Tjaša, and Polona Vilar. 2015. "Focus Group Interview through Storytelling." *Journal of Documentation* 71 (6): 1300–1316. doi:10.1108/JD-01-2015-0008.

Library Research Service. 2018. "Library User Survey Templates & How-Tos." https://www.lrs.org/library-user-surveys-on-the-web.

Lyons, Ray, and Keith Curry Lance. 2014. "LJ Index 2014: The Star Libraries." *Library Journal*, November 3. https://lj.libraryjournal.com/2014/11/managing-libraries/lj-index/class-of-2014/the-star-libraries-2014.

Matthews, Joseph. 2015. "Assessing Outcomes and Value: It's All a Matter of Perspective." *Performance Measurement and Metrics* 16 (3): 211–233. doi:10.1108/PMM-10-2015-0034.

Merriam, Sharan B., and Elizabeth J. Tisdell. 2016. *Qualitative Research: A Guide to Design and Implementation*. 4th ed. San Francisco: Jossey-Bass.

New York State Education Department. 2016. "NYSED School Library Media Program Evaluation Rubric." http://www.nysed.gov/school-library-services/nysed-school-library-media-program-evaluation-rubric.

Orr, R. H. 1973. "Measuring the Goodness of Library Services: A General Framework for Considering Quantitative Measures." *Journal of Documentation* 29 (3): 315–32. doi:10.1108/eb026561.

Priestley, Gina, and Margaret-Ellen Pipe. 1997. "Using Toys and Models in Interviews with Young Children." *Applied Cognitive Psychology* 11 (1): 69–87. doi:10.1002/(SICI)1099-0720(199702)11:13.0.CO;2-V.

Schindler, Esther, and Ross Rubin. 2018. "The Best Online Survey Tools of 2019." https://uk.pcmag.com/cloud-services/73249/the-best-online-survey-tools-of-2019.

South Dakota State Library. 2019. "21st Century School Library Self-Assessment." https://library.sd.gov/LIB/SLC/.

Walter, Virginia A. 1992. *Output Measures for Public Library Service to Children: A Manual of Standardized Procedures.* Chicago: American Library Association.

Woolls, Blanche. 2008. *The School Library Media Manager.* 4th ed. Westport, CT: Libraries Unlimited.

Chapter 2

Personnel

Many school librarians feel particularly isolated because they are the only one performing that job in their building. Whereas teachers can bounce ideas off of one another, most school librarians do not have the opportunity on a daily basis to interact with like-minded colleagues in their school. Because of this, you may have no idea how you or your programs compare with others.

This chapter on evaluation of personnel provides benchmarks of staffing and how school librarians are evaluated. Other personnel involved in school libraries are clerks and student aides. Several lists of questions are provided for interviewing and evaluating them.

BENCHMARKING

A national survey on staffing patterns in school libraries (National Center for Education Statistics 2012) furnishes baseline data on the number and percentages of full-time, part-time, and noncertified media specialists (school librarians) per state (figure 2.1). The next table (figure 2.2) is more descriptive in that schools are classified by whether they are public or private, the type of community they are in, student enrollment, and the percentage of students who are on free or reduced-price lunches. By comparing your school characteristics to those in the tables, you can get an idea as to whether your staffing is above or below national and state averages. For

Selected school characteristic	Total number of paid professional library media center staff[1]	Percent of paid professional library media center staff who were state-certified classroom teachers	Percent of paid professional library media center staff who had a master's degree in a library-related major[2]	Percent of paid professional library media center staff who are state-certified library media specialists	Total number of paid library aides or clerical staff	Total number of regularly scheduled volunteers (adult and student) during most recent full week
All public schools with library media centers	88,520	63.0	51.8	82.9	55,010	273,260
School classification						
Traditional public	86,340	63.6	52.5	83.6	54,180	266,070
Charter school	2,180	41.0	26.7	52.9	830	7,190
Community type						
City	22,080	61.1	50.5	81.0	12,030	72,050
Suburban	24,870	63.9	56.2	83.7	16,190	99,950
Town	11,780	62.9	49.1	83.1	8,190	29,260
Rural	29,790	63.8	50.2	83.5	18,600	72,010
School level						
Primary	50,000	60.3	48.5	81.7	30,560	181,080
Middle	14,630	67.9	58.2	87.2	9,470	49,060
High	18,240	68.5	60.2	85.4	12,130	36,050
Combined	5,640	56.3	38.0	73.9	2,850	7,060
Student enrollment						
Less than 100	2,770	57.7	37.5	76.7	2,060	3,450
100–199	5,960	46.8	31.6	74.1	3,210	5,400
200–499	35,870	62.9	49.1	82.5	20,650	106,130
500–749	22,650	62.7	54.0	82.6	13,920	83,820
750–999	9,560	69.2	56.0	85.1	6,640	37,010
1,000 or more	11,710	68.6	66.4	88.4	8,540	37,450
Percent of K–12 students who were approved for free or reduced-price lunches						
0–34	29,430	62.6	53.2	80.4	18,680	123,770
35–49	15,680	65.9	52.8	85.5	10,770	39,190
50–74	22,260	66.6	54.7	87.6	13,950	63,830
75 or more	19,970	57.9	46.7	80.2	10,650	40,770
School did not participate in free or reduced-price lunch program	1,180	55.7	39.5	65.5	950	5,690

[1] Paid professional library media center staff includes state-certified library media specialists and other professional staff with paid full-time or part-time positions in the library media center. Excludes library aides and clerical staff.

[2] A library-related major refers to degrees in librarianship, library science, information science, educational media, instructional design, or instructional technology.

NOTE: Percentages are based on the total number of paid professional library media center staff, including full-time and part-time. The 2011–12 Schools and Staffing Survey did not collect school library media center data from private schools. Detail may not sum to totals because of rounding.

Figure 2.1   Number and percentage distribution of library media centers that reported having full-time or part-time, state-certified, paid professional library media center specialists, by state: 2011–12

Source: U.S. Department of Education, National Center for Education Statistics, Schools and Staffing Survey (SASS), "Public School Library Media Center Data File," 2011–12.

example, if you are a school librarian in Oregon and working part-time, you are a member of a group of 23.1 percent in that state. That may seem like a lot, but Oregon also shows that 43.7 percent of their schools have no school librarians. Similarly, city schools have a slightly lower percentage (81 percent) compared to suburban (83.7 percent), town (83.1 percent), or rural (83.5 percent) schools. Keep in mind that these figures were published in 2012, which means they were collected a few years before that. Situations change, but the NCES statistics have remained relatively stable over the years they have been compiled.

ADMINISTRATORS' EVALUATION OF SCHOOL LIBRARIANS

With the introduction of the Common Core State Standards (CCSS) in 2009, along with other state- or district-level reforms, teacher evaluation became a hot topic in many school districts across the country (Moreillon 2013). Evaluation instruments for educators came under review, and this has been beneficial to school librarians because it provided the opportunity

Selected school characteristic	Total number of schools[1]	Number of public schools with a library media center[2]
All public schools	90,000	81,200
School classification		
Traditional public	85,500	79,000
Charter school	4,500	2,200
Community type		
City	23,600	20,200
Suburban	24,300	22,500
Town	12,200	11,000
Rural	29,900	27,500
School level		
Primary	50,300	47,400
Middle	14,000	13,400
High	18,400	15,400
Combined	7,400	5,000
Student enrollment		
Less than 100	6,800	3,600
100-199	6,500	5,100
200-499	37,100	34,200
500-749	21,700	20,800
750-999	8,900	8,600
1,000 or more	9,100	8,800
Percent of K-12 students who were approved for free or reduced-price lunches		
0-34	27,000	25,700
35-49	14,600	14,000
50-74	23,000	21,300
75 or more	22,100	18,800
School did not participate in free or reduced-price lunch program	3,300	1,400

[1] The Public School Data File was used to generate these estimates, which are rounded to hundreds.

[2] The Public School Library Media Center Data File was used to generate these estimates, which are rounded to hundreds.

NOTE: The 2011–12 Schools and Staffing Survey did not collect school library media center data from private schools. Detail may not sum to totals because of rounding.

Figure 2.2 Number of public schools that reported having library media centers by selected school characteristics: 2011–2012

Source: U.S. Department of Education, National Center for Education Statistics, Schools and Staffing Survey (SASS), "Public School Library Media Center Data File," 2011–12.

to develop instruments that more closely align with the numerous roles they performed. Previously, and what is still the case in many schools, school librarians' performance was assessed exclusively on the teaching role without regard to program administrator, leader, instructional partner, or information specialist roles (Elkins 2014). Multitudes of school systems have adopted the Framework for Teaching by the Danielson Group (2018) for teacher evaluation, thus stimulating state and local professional groups of school librarians to modify the instrument for use in the school library. This alignment of the evaluation of school librarians and classroom teachers can facilitate understanding of school librarians' various roles by the evaluators and also teacher colleagues. Figure 2.3 shows a Danielson adaptation that was designed by the Association for Indiana School Library Educators (AISLE).

Association of Indiana School Library Educators

School Librarian Evaluation Rubric

This document in its entirety is endorsed by the Association for Indiana School Library Educators (AISLE). Any changes must be approved by the local school administration and the Indiana Department of Education. Please contact Robyn Young (rryoung@avon-schools.org) or Denise Keogh (dkeogh@tcsc.k12.in.us) for questions specific to this rubric.

It is recommended that this evaluation tool be used at the school library where the majority of the librarian's time is spent.

Approved by the AISLE Board November 14, 2012   Copyright 2012

Figure 2.3   Danielson Framework
Source: Reprinted with permission of the Association for Indiana School Library Educators (AISLE)

AISLE School Librarian Evaluation Rubric
Allowable Modifications to the School Librarian Evaluation Rubric

It is recommended that this document be used in its entirety as it is best practice for a school librarian. The following minor edits do not require permission from AISLE:

- Use of the rubric with all domains and competencies
- Addition of competencies
- Notes added to clarify the domains or competencies

The rubric should not be changed to fit the current job description of the school librarian, but the rubric should be followed as an example of best practice in the field of school librarians.

Expected levels of Competency – Use established weights below when using the School Librarian Evaluation Rubric. While all domains and competencies must be included, these weights may be changed by individual schools; however, no Domain may fall below 25%.

Domain 1	30%
Domain 2	40 %
Domain 3	30%

It is expected that School Librarians will follow the percentages of the Group 3 teachers with no growth model classes posted in the original RISE document; however, this may be changed within each school corporation if the SLO is not used.

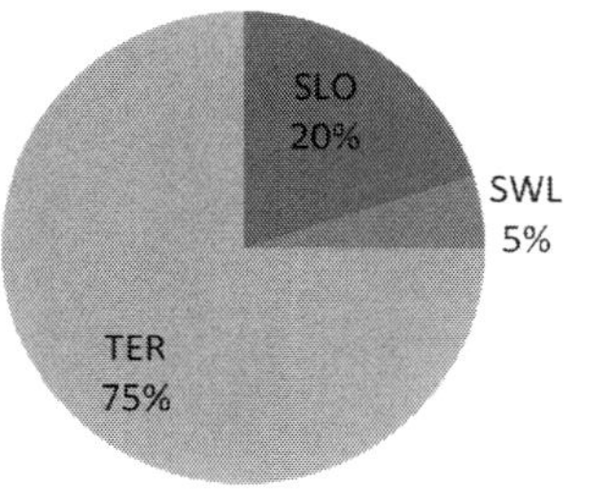

TER=Teacher Effectiveness Rubric (School Librarian Rubric)
SLO=Student Learning Objective
SWL=School-Wide Learning Measure

Approved by the AISLE Board November 14, 2012

Figure 2.3 Continued

AISLE School Librarian Evaluation Rubric

SLO Options for School Librarians

From the Indiana Department of Education:

Under the Indiana evaluation law (Indiana Code 20-28-11.5), which governs all certificated employee evaluations, *no one is required to use SLOs*. What *is required* is that objective measures of student achievement must *significantly inform* the evaluation of each certificated employee. The law does not define "significant", and local school corporations need to define what "significant" looks like in the summative evaluation metrics for their employees.

In RISE, which is the optional state model for teacher evaluation, classroom teachers are required to set SLOs. Please note, the RISE teacher evaluation and development system was really designed to evaluate classroom teachers, and not specifically designed to evaluate other professionals in the schools who are not specifically assigned students. You can choose to use or modify RISE with other employees, but you can also choose to use other rubrics, student learning measures, summative metrics, etc. with your non-teacher employees (as long as the evaluation complies with law), and you're still considered a RISE school for teacher evaluations.

SLOs were designed to be the mechanism through which objective measures of student achievement can be captured for those teachers without mandatory state assessment data coming back to them. We would encourage the use of SLOs with any certificated employee whose responsibilities include direct work with students that would impact student learning and achievement. For school librarians, you might consider setting two Targeted objectives, or utilizing the administrative SLO format described in the RISE principal evaluation documents. Those SLO formats seem to "fit" better with school librarians than the "one Class and one Targeted" SLO format.

If, however, a certificated employee truly doesn't do any work that can be tied directly back to student learning and data, they are not required to set an SLO. In these cases, we would encourage you to carefully consider how you will include objective measures of student learning for that employee, and what "significant" means for them. For example, you might consider how to weight a school-wide learning measure (A-F grade) for those employees. You also might consider asking these employees to set SMART goals around the work for which they're responsible, even if the end measurement isn't a student learning measure.

Approved by the AISLE Board November 14, 2012

Figure 2.3 Continued

The School Librarian Evaluation Rubric is an extremely effective measure of performance by a school librarian. It is required that all domains be used.

To measure a librarian's effect on student learning, a variety of scenarios may occur:

- As the evaluation rubric is comprehensive, the principal may choose to use the evaluation rubric as 95% of the evaluation, with 5% coming from the school-wide measure of student learning and not complete an SLO as measures of learning are built into the evaluation rubric.
- If a librarian consistently collaborates with a classroom teacher on a project, the student learning on that project may be used as a measure of evaluation for the school librarian.
- If a school librarian has students assigned to him/her and are responsible for providing grades for the students, that group of students may be used for the SLO.

Any of these options may be used, but the school librarian should not focus on a contrived set of goals in order to meet the SLO. It should be a part of the regular job responsibilities of the school librarian (i.e. librarians should not be teaching a science class just to make an SLO).

Domain 1: Purposeful Planning

Approved by the AISLE Board November 14, 2012

Figure 2.3 Continued

AISLE School Librarian Evaluation Rubric

School librarians work in collaboration with the classroom teacher to develop a rigorous curriculum relevant for all students. Additionally, school librarians will plan the library media program for the school.

Level of Performance				
Competencies	Highly Effective (4)	Effective (3)	Improvement Necessary (2)	Ineffective (1)
1.1 **Demonstrating knowledge of literature and current trends in library practice and information technology**	Drawing on extensive professional resources, school librarian demonstrates rich understanding of literature and of current trends in information technology. *- Librarian maintains a network of professional contacts and resources to stay current with trends (this includes reading current journals, blogs, and using social media) and shares with staff and students.*	School librarian demonstrates thorough knowledge of literature and of current trends in practice and information technology. *- Librarian maintains a professional network to stay current with trends. This includes reading current journals, blogs, and using social media.*	School librarian demonstrates limited knowledge of literature and current trends in practice and information technology. *- Librarian reads journals to learn about current trends.*	School librarian demonstrates little or no knowledge of literature and of current trends in practice and information technology.
Notes 1.1 1. Extensive professional resources may include, but is not limited to, blogs, Twitter, Facebook or other social media, professional journals, conferences and webinars, professional contacts with authors or other library professionals. 2. Current trends – librarian is aware of changes in library practice and is actively pursuing, implementing or further investigating these changes to see the benefit for the library.				

Approved by the AISLE Board November 14, 2012   Copyright 2012

Figure 2.3   Continued

AISLE School Librarian Evaluation Rubric

	Competencies	Level of Performance			
		Highly Effective (4)	Effective (3)	Improvement Necessary (2)	Ineffective (1)
1.2	**Establishing and successfully implementing goals for the school library program appropriate to the setting and the students served**	School librarian's goals for the media program are highly appropriate to the situation in the school and to the age of the students and have been developed following consultations with students and colleagues -*The goal for the program is communicated with appropriate stakeholders with regular assessments to determine if goal is being met.*	School librarian's goals for the media program are clear and appropriate to the situation in the school and to the age of the students. -*The goal for the program is communicated with appropriate stakeholders.*	School librarian's goals for the media program are rudimentary and are partially suitable to the situation in the school and the age of the students. - *The goal for the program is established by not communicated with appropriate stakeholders.*	School librarian has no clear goals for the media program or they are inappropriate to either the situation in the school or the age of the students.
	Notes 1.2 1. Goals may be shared verbally or written; however, it is important that the goal be shared with the learning community. This may include staff, students, administrators or community members.				
1.3	**Demonstrating knowledge of resources, both within and beyond the school and district**	School librarian shows evidence of resources available for students and teachers and actively seeks out new resources from a wide range of sources to enrich the school's program.	School librarian shows evidence of resources available for students and teachers in the school, in other schools in the district, and in the larger community to enrich the school's program.	School librarian demonstrates basic knowledge of resources available for students and teachers in the school, in other schools in the district, and in the larger community to enrich the school's program.	School librarian demonstrates little or no knowledge of resources available for students and teachers in the school, in other schools in the district, and in the larger community to enrich the school's program.
	Notes 1.3 1. This competency refers to knowledge of the library collection and finding information for staff and students. The evidence may include, but is not limited to, the school library book collection, using interlibrary loan, internet sources, database sources, or the use of the public library collection. A highly effective librarian will use many of these resources to provide information for staff or students.				

Approved by the AISLE Board November 14, 2012

Figure 2.3 Continued

AISLE School Librarian Evaluation Rubric

		Level of Performance			
	Competencies	Highly Effective (4)	Effective (3)	Improvement Necessary (2)	Ineffective (1)
1.4	**Developing and implementing a plan to evaluate the library program**	School librarian's evaluation plan is highly sophisticated, with imaginative sources of evidence and a clear path toward improving the program on an ongoing basis. - The librarian proactively responds to the evidence of the evaluation.	School librarian's plan to evaluate the program is organized around clear goals and the collection of evidence to indicate the degree to which the goals have been met.	School librarian has a rudimentary plan to evaluate the library program.	School librarian has no plan to evaluate the program or resists suggestions that such an evaluation is important.
	Notes 1.4 1. Some sources of evidence may include student and staff surveys, assessment documents, and statistical data.				
1.5	**Establishing a culture for investigation and love of literature**	In interactions with both students and colleagues, the school librarian conveys the essential nature of seeking information and reading literature.	In interactions with both students and colleagues, the school librarian conveys the importance of seeking information and reading literature.	School librarian goes through the motions of performing the work of the position, but without any real commitment to it.	School librarian conveys that the work of seeking information and reading literature is not worth the time and energy required.
1.6	**Establishing and maintaining library procedures**	Library routines and procedures (for example, circulation of materials, collection development policy, challenged materials form, students working independent within the library) are seamless in their operation.	Library routines and procedures (for example, circulation of materials, collection development policy, challenged materials form, students working independent within the library) have been established and function smoothly.	Library routines and procedures (for example, circulation of materials, collection development policy, challenged materials form, students working independent within the library) have been established but function sporadically.	Library routines and procedures (for example, circulation of materials, collection development policy, challenged materials form, students working independent within the library) are either non-existent or inefficient, resulting in general confusion.

Approved by the AISLE Board November 14, 2012

Figure 2.3   Continued

AISLE School Librarian Evaluation Rubric

		Level of Performance			
	Competencies	Highly Effective (4)	Effective (3)	Improvement Necessary (2)	Ineffective (1)
1.7	Organize physical space to enable smooth flow	School librarian makes highly effective use of the physical environment, resulting in clear signage, excellent traffic flow, and adequate space devoted to work areas and computer use. In addition, book displays are attractive and inviting.	School librarian makes effective use of the physical environment, resulting in good traffic flow, clear signage, and adequate space devoted to work areas and computer use.	School librarian's efforts to make use of the physical environment are uneven, resulting in occasional confusion by users.	School librarian makes poor use of the physical environment, resulting in poor traffic flow, confusing signage, inadequate space devoted to work areas and computer use, and general confusion.
	Notes 1.7 1. Smooth flow is defined as students and staff being able to function within the library easily and independently based upon location of materials, signs, and seating.				
1.8	Maintaining and extending the library collection in accordance with the schools' needs and within budget limitations	School librarian adheres to district or professional guidelines in selecting materials for the collection. The collection is periodically purged of outdated materials. A virtual collection is maintained and updated frequently by the librarian is vibrant and well-used. All processes are done in consultation with teaching colleagues or patron needs in mind.	School librarian adheres to district or professional guidelines in selecting materials for the collection and periodically purges the collection of outdated materials. A virtual collection is maintained by the librarian. This is done in some consultation with teaching colleagues or patron needs in mind.	School librarian is partially successful in attempts to adhere to district or professional guidelines in selecting materials and in weeding the collection. A virtual presence may not be maintained. This is done in limited consultation with teaching colleagues or with patron needs in mind.	School librarian fails to adhere to district or professional guidelines in selecting materials for the collection and does not periodically purge the collection of outdated material. There is no virtual presence. This is done without consultation with teaching colleagues or with patron needs in mind.
	Notes 1.8 1. The librarian will maintain the school's collection with many factors of the school's needs in mind. The librarian will support the curriculum and the school's academic needs, as well as the practice of reading (for enjoyment or for information). Additionally, this may include a digital collection.				

Approved by the AISLE Board November 14, 2012

Copyright 2012

35

Figure 2.3 Continued

AISLE School Librarian Evaluation Rubric

Domain 2: Effective Instruction

Librarians, working collaboratively with classroom teachers, facilitate student academic practice so that all students are participating and have the opportunity to gain mastery of the objectives. The librarian fosters a climate of urgency and expectation around achievement, excellence and respect.

For Competencies 2.2 through 2.5, in order to be highly effective, each competency says that the librarian must show some of the following indicators. We define "some" as at least one. All of the indicators under effective may not be shown in one observation, but should be shown throughout the observation cycle.

		Level of Performance			
	Competencies	Highly Effective (4)	Effective (3)	Improvement Necessary (2)	Ineffective (1)
2.1	**Creating an environment conducive to learning**	Interactions among the school librarian, individual students, and the classroom teachers are highly respectful, reflecting genuine warmth and caring and sensitivity to students' learning needs, cultures and levels of development.	Interactions between the school librarian, students, and the classroom teachers, are polite and respectful, reflecting general warmth and caring, and are appropriate to the learning needs, cultural and developmental differences among students.	Interactions between the school librarian, students, and the classroom teachers are generally appropriate and free from conflict but may be characterized by occasional displays of insensitivity or lack of responsiveness to learning needs, cultural and developmental differences among students.	Interactions between the school librarian, students, and the classroom teachers are negative, inappropriate, or insensitive to students' learning needs, cultural and developmental differences and are characterized by sarcasm, put-downs or conflict.

Approved by the AISLE Board November 14, 2012

Copyright 2012

Figure 2.3   Continued

AISLE School Librarian Evaluation Rubric

2.2	**Demonstrate and Clearly Communicate Content Knowledge to Students**	School librarian is highly effective at demonstrating and clearly communicating content knowledge to students. For Level 4, all of the evidence listed under Level 3 is present, as well as some of the following: *- Librarian fully explains concepts in as direct and efficient a manner as possible, while still achieving student understanding* *- Librarian effectively connects content to other content areas, students' experiences and interests, or current events in order to make content relevant and build interest* *- Explanations spark student excitement and interest in the content* *- Students participate in each others' learning of content through collaboration during the lesson* *- Students ask higher-order questions and make connections independently, demonstrating that they understand the content at a higher level*	School librarian is effective at demonstrating and clearly communicating content knowledge to students. Librarian demonstrates content knowledge and delivers content that is factually correct *- Content is clear, concise and well-organized* *- Librarian restates and rephrases instruction in multiple ways to increase understanding* *- Librarian emphasizes key points or main ideas in content* *- Librarian uses developmentally appropriate language and explanations* *- Librarian implements relevant instructional strategies learned via professional development*	School librarian needs improvement at demonstrating and clearly communicating content knowledge to students. Librarian delivers content that is factually correct *- Content occasionally lacks clarity and is not as well organized as it could be* *- Librarian may fail to restate or rephrase instruction in multiple ways to increase understanding* *- Librarian does not adequately emphasize main ideas, and students are sometimes confused about key takeaways* *- Explanations sometimes lack developmentally appropriate language* *- Librarian does not always implement new and improved instructional strategies learned via professional development*	School librarian is ineffective at demonstrating and clearly communicating content knowledge to students. *-Librarian may deliver content that is factually incorrect* *- Explanations may be unclear or incoherent and fail to build student understanding of key concepts* *- Librarian continues with planned instruction, even when it is obvious that students are not understanding content* *- Librarian does not emphasize main ideas, and students are often confused about content* *- Librarian fails to use developmentally appropriate language*
	Notes 2.2 1. Content may be communicated by either direct instruction or guided inquiry depending on the context of the classroom or lesson.				

Figure 2.3   Continued

AISLE School Librarian Evaluation Rubric

2.3	Engage Students in Academic Content	Librarian is highly effective at engaging students in academic content	Librarian is effective at engaging students in academic content	Librarian needs improvement at engaging students in academic content	Librarian is ineffective at engaging students in academic content
		For Level 4, all of the evidence listed under Level 3 is present, as well as some of the following: - Librarian provides ways to engage with content that significantly promotes student mastery of the objective - Librarian provides differentiated ways of engaging with content specific to individual student needs - The lesson progresses at an appropriate pace so that students are never disengaged, and students who finish early have something else meaningful to do - Librarian effectively integrates technology as a tool to engage students in academic content	-More than 3/4 of students are actively engaged in content at all times and not off-task -Librarian provides multiple ways, as appropriate, of engaging with content, all aligned to the lesson objective - Librarian sustains the attention of the class by maintaining a dynamic presence - Ways of engaging with content reflect different learning modalities or intelligences - Librarian adjusts lesson accordingly to accommodate for student prerequisite skills and knowledge so that all students are engaged - ELL and IEP students have the appropriate accommodations to be engaged in content - Students work hard and are deeply active rather than passive/receptive (See Notes below for specific evidence of engagement)	- Fewer than 3/4 of students are engaged in content and many are off-task - Librarian may provide multiple ways of engaging students, but perhaps not aligned to lesson objective or mastery of content - Librarian may miss opportunities to provide ways of differentiating content for student engagement - Some students may not have the prerequisite skills necessary to fully engage in content and Librarian's attempt to modify instruction for these students is limited or not always effective - Students may appear to actively listen, but when it comes time for participation are disinterested in engaging	- Fewer than 1/2 of students are engaged in content and many are off-task - Librarian may only provide one way of engaging with content OR Librarian may provide multiple ways of engaging students that are not aligned to the lesson objective or mastery of content - Librarian does not differentiate instruction to target different learning modalities - Most students do not have the prerequisite skills necessary to fully engage in content and Librarian makes no effort to adjust instruction for these students - ELL and IEP students are not provided with the necessary accommodations to engage in content

Figure 2.3   Continued

AISLE School Librarian Evaluation Rubric

Notes 2.3
1. The most important indicator of success here is that students are actively engaged in the content. For a teacher to receive credit for providing students a way of engaging with content, students must be engaged in that part of the lesson.
2. Presence can best be represented by using engaging, confident, and assertive body language, tone, volume, and proximity.
3. Engagement is defined as on-task behavior. Some observable evidence of engagement may include (but is not limited to): (a) raising of hands to ask and answer questions as well as to share ideas; (b) active listening (not off-task) during lesson; or (c) active participation in hands-on tasks/activities.
4. Teachers may provide multiple ways of engaging with content via different learning modalities (auditory, visual, kinesthetic/tactile) or via multiple intelligences (spatial, linguistic, musical, interpersonal, logical-mathematical, etc). It may also be effective to engage students via two or more strategies targeting the same modality.

Approved by the AISLE Board November 14, 2012

Copyright 2012

Figure 2.3 Continued

AISLE School Librarian Evaluation Rubric

2.4	Check for Understanding	School librarian is highly effective at checking for understanding.	School librarian is effective at checking for understanding.	School librarian needs improvement at checking for understanding.	School librarian is ineffective at checking for understanding.
		For Level 4, all of the evidence listed under Level 3 is present, as well as some of the following: - Librarian checks for understanding at higher levels by asking pertinent, scaffold questions that push thinking; accepts only high quality student responses (those that reveal understanding or lack thereof) - Librarian uses open-ended questions to surface common misunderstandings and assess student mastery of material at a range of both lower and higher-order thinking	- Librarian checks for understanding at almost all key moments (when checking is necessary to inform instruction going forward) and gets an accurate "pulse" of the class's understanding - Librarian gains enough information during checks for understanding to modify the lesson and respond accordingly - Librarian uses a variety of methods to check for understanding - Librarian uses wait time effectively both after posing a question and before helping students think through a response - Librarian doesn't allow students to "opt-out" of checks for understanding and cycles back to these students - Librarian systematically assesses every student's mastery of the objective(s) at the end of each lesson through formal or informal assessments (see note for examples)	- Librarian sometimes checks for understanding of content, but misses several key moments - Librarian mostly gets an accurate "pulse" of the class's understanding, but may not gain enough information to modify the lesson accordingly - Librarian may not use a variety of methods to check for understanding when doing so would be helpful - Librarian may not provide enough wait time after posing a question for students to think and respond before helping with an answer or moving forward with content - Librarian sometimes allows students to "opt-out" of checks for understanding without cycling back to these students - Librarian may assess student mastery at the end of the lesson through formal or informal assessments, but may not use this information to drive subsequent lesson planning	- Librarian rarely or never checks for understanding of content, or misses nearly all key moments - Librarian rarely or never gets an accurate "pulse" of the class's understanding from checks and therefore cannot gain enough information to modify the lesson - Librarian frequently moves on with content before students have a chance to respond to questions or frequently gives students the answer rather than helping them think through the answer - Librarian frequently allows students to "opt-out" of checks for understanding and does not cycle back to these students - Librarian rarely or never assesses for mastery at the end of the lesson

Figure 2.3 Continued

AISLE School Librarian Evaluation Rubric

	Notes 2.4 1. Examples of times when checking for understanding may be useful are: before moving on to the next step of the lesson, or partway through independent practice. 2. Examples of how the teacher may assess student understanding and mastery of objectives: · Checks for Understanding: thumbs up/down, cold-calling ·Do Nows/Bell Ringers Turn and Talk/Pair Share · Guided or Independent Practice · Exit Slips				
2.5	**Modify Instruction as Needed**	School librarian is highly effective at modifying instruction as needed. For Level 4, all of the evidence listed under Level 3 is present, as well as some of the following: - Librarian anticipates student misunderstandings and preemptively addresses them - Librarian is able to modify instruction to respond to misunderstandings without taking away from the flow of the lesson or losing engagement	School librarian is effective at modifying instruction as needed. - Librarian makes adjustments to instruction based on checks for understanding that lead to increased understanding for most students - Librarian differentiates delivery of instruction based on checks for understanding and assessment data to meet diverse student needs - Librarian responds to misunderstandings with effective scaffolding techniques - Librarian doesn't give up, but continues to try to address misunderstanding with different techniques if the first try is not successful	School librarian needs improvement at modifying instruction as needed. - Librarian may attempt to make adjustments based on checks for understanding, but these attempts may be misguided and may not increase understanding for all students - Librarian may primarily respond to misunderstandings by using teacher-driven scaffolding techniques (for example, re-explaining a concept), when student-driven techniques could have been more effective - Librarian may persist in using a particular technique for responding to a misunderstanding, even when it is not succeeding	School librarian is ineffective at modifying instruction as needed. - Librarian rarely or never attempts to adjust instruction based on checks for understanding, and any attempts at doing so frequently fail to increase understanding for students - Librarian only responds to misunderstandings by using teacher-driven scaffolding techniques - Librarian repeatedly uses the same techniques to respond to misunderstandings, even when it is not succeeding

Approved by the AISLE Board November 14, 2012

Figure 2.3   Continued

AISLE School Librarian Evaluation Rubric

2.6	**Maximize Instructional Time**	School librarian is highly effective at maximizing instructional time. For Level 4, all of the evidence listed under Level 3 is present, as well as the following: - All students are on-task and follow instructions of Librarian without much prompting	School librarian is effective at maximizing instructional time. - Routines, transitions, and procedures are well-executed. - Almost all students are on-task and follow instructions of librarian without much prompting - Disruptive behaviors and off-task conversations are rare; when they occur, they are almost always addressed without major interruption to the lesson	School librarian needs improvement at maximizing instructional time. - Routines, transitions, and procedures are in place. - Significant prompting from the librarian is necessary for students to follow instructions and remain on-task - Disruptive behaviors and off-task conversations sometimes occur; they may not be addressed in the most effective manner and Librarian may have to stop the lesson frequently to address the problem	School librarian is ineffective at maximizing instructional time. - There are few or no evident routines or procedures in place. - Even with significant prompting, students frequently do not follow directions and are off-task - Disruptive behaviors and off-task conversations are common and frequently cause the librarian to have to make adjustments to the lesson - Classroom management is generally poor and wastes instructional time
2.7	**Assisting students in the use of technology in the Media Center**	School librarian proactively initiates sessions to assist students and teachers in the use of technology.	School librarian institutes sessions to assist students and teachers in the use of technology.	School librarian assists students and teachers in the use of technology when specifically asked to do so.	School librarian declines to assist students and teachers in the use of technology.
	Notes 2.7 1. The overall indicator of success here is that operationally, the library runs smoothly so that time can be spent on valuable instruction rather than logistics and discipline. 2. It should be understood that a teacher can have disruptive students no matter how effective he/she may be. However, an effective teacher should be able to minimize disruptions amongst these students and when they do occur, handle them without detriment to the learning of other students.				
2.8	**Collaborating with teachers in the design of instructional units and lessons**	School librarian initiates collaboration with classroom teachers in the design of instructional lessons, locating additional resources from sources outside of the school.	School librarian initiates collaboration with classroom teachers in the design of instructional lessons.	School librarian collaborates with classroom teachers in the design of instructional lessons.	School librarian declines to collaborate with classroom teachers in the design of instructional lessons.

Approved by the AISLE Board November 14, 2012   Copyright 2012

Figure 2.3 Continued

AISLE School Librarian Evaluation Rubric

2.9	Engaging students in enjoying literature and in learning multiple literacy skills	Students are highly engaged in enjoying literature and in learning information skills because of effective design of activities, grouping strategies, and appropriate materials.	Students are engaged in enjoying literature and in learning information skills because of effective design of activities, grouping strategies, and appropriate materials.	Only some students are engaged in enjoying literature and in learning information skills because of uneven design of activities, grouping strategies, or partially appropriate materials.	Students are not engaged in enjoying literature and in learning information skills because of poor design of activities, poor grouping strategies, or inappropriate materials.

Approved by the AISLE Board November 14, 2012

Figure 2.3 Continued

AISLE School Librarian Evaluation Rubric

Domain 3: Leadership

Teachers develop and sustain the intense energy and leadership within their school community to ensure the achievement of all students.

	Competencies	Level of Performance			
		Highly Effective (4)	Effective (3)	Improvement Necessary (2)	Ineffective (1)
3.1	Contribute to school culture	School librarian seeks out leadership roles within the school, aimed at improving school efforts. Librarian goes above and beyond in dedicating time for students and peers outside of class.	School librarian contributes ideas and expertise aimed at improving school efforts. Librarian dedicates time efficiently, when needed, to helping students and peers outside of class.	School librarian will rarely contribute ideas and expertise aimed at improving school efforts. Librarian rarely dedicates time outside of class to helping students and peers.	School librarian never contributes ideas aimed at improving school efforts. Little or no time outside of class is dedicated to helping students and peers.
	Notes 3.1 1. An effective librarian participates in school events that make a substantial contribution above classroom expectations whereas a highly effective librarian additionally assumes a leadership role in at least one aspect of school life.				
3.2	Collaborate with Peers	School librarian will go above and beyond in seeking out opportunities to collaborate. Librarian will coach peers through difficult situations and take on leadership roles within collaborative groups such as Professional Learning Communities.	School librarian will seek out and participate in regular opportunities to work with and learn from others. Librarian will ask for assistance, when needed, and provide assistance to others in need.	School librarian will participate in occasional opportunities to work with and learn from others and ask for assistance when needed. Librarian will not seek to provide other teachers with assistance when needed or will not regularly seek out opportunities to work with others.	School librarian rarely or never participates in opportunities to work with others. Librarian works in isolation and is not a team player.
	Notes 3.2 1. The main purpose of collaboration with peers is to support the curriculum. 2. A highly effective librarian will seek out opportunities to collaborate, whereas an effective librarian may collaborate when asked. 3. An effective librarian builds relationships with colleagues that are characterized by mutual support and cooperation whereas a highly effective librarian additionally takes initiatives in assuming leadership among the faculty.				
3.3	Establishing, evaluating, and maintaining library procedures in regards to staffing, student or parent volunteers	Library assistants, students, or parent/community volunteers work independently and contribute to the success of the library. -The librarian will proactively evaluate procedures.	Library assistants, students, or parent/community volunteers are clear as to their roles.	Library assistants, students, or parent/community volunteers are partially successful.	Library assistants, students, or parent/community volunteers are confused as to their role.

Approved by the AISLE Board November 14, 2012

Figure 2.3   Continued

AISLE School Librarian Evaluation Rubric

3.4	**Advocate for Student Success**	School librarian will display commitment to the education of the students in the school, not just his/her own students. Librarian will make changes and take risks to ensure student success and advocate for students' individualized needs.	School librarian will display commitment to the education of his/her students. Librarian will attempt to remedy obstacles around student achievement and will advocate for students' individualized needs.	School librarian will display commitment to the education of his/her students. School librarian will not advocate for students' needs.	School librarian rarely or never displays commitment to the education of his/her students. Librarian accepts failure as par for the course and does not advocate for students' needs.
3.5	**Preparing and submitting reports and budgets**	School librarian anticipates student and teacher needs when preparing requisitions and budgets, follows established procedures, and suggests improvements to those procedures. Inventories and reports are submitted on time.	School librarian honors student and teacher requests (if appropriate) when preparing requisitions and budgets and follows established procedures. Inventories and reports are submitted on time.	School librarian's efforts to prepare budgets are partially successful, responding sometimes to student and teacher requests (if appropriate) and following procedures. Inventories and reports are sometimes submitted on time.	School librarian ignores student and teacher requests (if appropriate) when preparing requisitions and budgets or does not follow established procedures. Inventories and reports are routinely late.
3.6	**Communicating with the larger community**	School librarian proactively reaches out to parents and establishes contacts with other libraries or businesses, coordinating efforts for mutual benefit.	School librarian engages in outreach efforts to parents and the larger community.	School librarian makes sporadic efforts to engage in outreach to parents or the larger community.	School librarian makes no effort to engage in outreach to parents or the larger community.
3.7	**Participating in a professional community**	School librarian makes a substantial contribution to school and district events and projects and assumes leadership with colleagues. Librarian participates and develops leadership roles in a wider professional community that includes local, state, or national events.	School librarian participates actively in school and district events and projects and maintains positive and productive relationships with colleagues. Librarian will participate in a wider professional community that includes local, state, or national contacts.	School librarian's relationships with colleagues are cordial, and the librarian participates in school and district events when specifically requested.	School librarian's relationships with colleagues are negative or self-serving, and the librarian avoids being involved in school and district events and projects.
3.8	**Seek professional skills and knowledge**	School librarian actively pursues professional development opportunities and makes a substantial contribution to the profession through such activities as sharing newly learned knowledge and practices with others and seeking out opportunities to lead professional development sessions.	School librarian actively pursues opportunities to improve knowledge and practice and seeks out ways to implement new practices where applicable. Constructive feedback to improve practices is welcomed.	School librarian's participation in professional development activities is limited to those that are mandatory.	School librarian does not participate in professional development activities, and shows little or no interest in new ideas, programs, or classes to improve teaching and learning.

Approved by the AISLE Board November 14, 2012

Figure 2.3   Continued

AISLE School Librarian Evaluation Rubric

Notes 3.8	
	1. An effective librarian seeks and implements professional skills and knowledge whereas a highly effective librarian additionally shares and facilitates this information with colleagues regularly.

Approved by the AISLE Board November 14, 2012

Figure 2.3 Continued

AISLE School Librarian Evaluation Rubric

Domain 4: Core Professionalism

These indicators illustrate the minimum competencies expected in any profession. These are separate from other sections in the rubric because they have little to do with teaching and learning and more to do with basic employment practice. Teachers are expected to meet these standards. If they do not, it will affect their overall rating negatively.

Indicator		Does Not Meet Standard	Meets Standard
1	Attendance	Individual demonstrates a pattern of unexcused absences.*	Individual has not demonstrated a pattern of unexcused absences.*
2	On-Time Arrival	Individual demonstrates a pattern of unexcused late arrivals (late arrivals that are in violation of procedures set forth by local school policy and by the relevant collective bargaining agreement).	Individual has not demonstrated a pattern of unexcused late arrivals (late arrivals that are in violation of procedures set forth by local school policy and by the relevant collective bargaining agreement).
3	Policies and Procedures	Individual demonstrates a pattern of failing to follow state, corporation, and school policies and procedures (e.g. procedures for submitting discipline referrals, policies for appropriate attire, etc.)	Individual demonstrates a pattern of following state, corporation, and school policies and procedures (e.g. procedures for submitting discipline referrals, policies for appropriate attire, etc.)
4	Respect	Individual demonstrates a pattern of failing to interact with students, colleagues, parents/guardians, and community members in a respectful manner.	Individual demonstrates a pattern of interacting with students, colleagues, parents/guardians, and community members in a respectful manner.

*It should be left to the discretion of the corporation to define "unexcused absence" in this context.

1. Complying with policies and procedures includes but is not limited to: Following IEP/504 plans, complying with discipline referral processes, parent communication expectations (typically e-mails or phone calls returned by within 24 hours during the work week), providing sub plans, implementing school rules, maintaining accurate, up-to-date records, and dressing professionally. The sub-committee recommends discussion of dress code expectations. Establishing clear expectations about jeans, flip-flops, revealing attire, etc. will be important for consistency.

2. Demonstrating respect to students, parents and colleagues includes maintaining appropriate (not too familiar) boundaries. Respectfully listening to negative feedback and maintaining emotional self control even in heated situations is expected. Accepting constructive criticism is a hallmark of this standard.

3. It is understood that if an administrator has a concern about a teacher not meeting these standards, it will be called to the attention of the teacher as soon as possible so correction can ensue.

Approved by the AISLE Board November 14, 2012 — Copyright 2012

Figure 2.3 Continued

AISLE School Librarian Evaluation Rubric

Works Cited

Danielson, Charlotte. *Enhancing professional practice: a framework for teaching.* 2nd ed. Alexandria, Va.: Association for Supervision and Curriculum Development, 2007. Print.

Empowering learners: guidelines for school library media programs. Chicago, Ill.: American Association of School Librarians, 2009. Print.

RISE INDIANA. N.p., n.d. Web. 12 Jan. 2012. <http://www.riseindiana.org>.

Approved by the AISLE Board November 14, 2012

Copyright 2012

Figure 2.3 Continued

After an observation using the Danielson Framework (Danielson Group 2018), principals are likely to engage in conversation with the librarian to determine strengths and areas for improvement. To be prepared for this exchange, you might consult the possible guiding questions for principals and potential responses by librarians that have been prepared by the Pennsylvania Department of Education (2013). Here are a few examples:

Domain 1: Planning and Preparation
- How do you develop collaborative and/or differentiated instruction?
  - *Collaboration is developed through communication with the content area teacher(s), joint planning of lessons/assessments and a variety of resources to meet student needs.*

Domain 2: The Classroom Environment
- How do you utilize the existing physical space to maximize student learning?
  - *The physical layout of the library is flexible to accommodate technology, large group instruction, collaborative groups, individual instruction, literacy activities, etc. Displays promote reading and information literacy. Materials are accessible to all students.*

Domain 3: Instruction
- How do you know that your instruction is effective?
  - *Students are on task. Teacher/librarian reflection meetings on the success of a project. Student reflections. Observation, students met teacher's or librarian's objective.*

Domain 4: Professional Responsibilities
- What professional development contributed to the strategies you used during the lesson?
  - *Possible answers may include use of new technologies/strategies learned during conferences, in-services, webinars, and professional journal reviews of new resources.*

In a study conducted by this author (Everhart 2006), it was found that principals consult a variety of evidence when evaluating their school librarians. Of fourteen possible sources of information for evaluative purposes, each received varying degrees of use. A ranking of principals' most frequent types of evaluation is found in table 2.1.

Principals said they evaluate their school librarians most frequently by informally visiting the school library. When principals visit informally,

Table 2-1 Principals' Most Frequent Type of School Librarian Evaluation

	Weekly		Monthly		Once per Semester		Once per Year		Never		Weighted Ranking	Total
	n	%	n	%	n	%	n	%	n	%		
1. Informal visits	57	89.1%	7	10.9%	0	0.0%	0	0.0%	0	0.0%	313	100%
2. Examine student work	30	46.9%	26	40.6%	0	0.0%	5	7.8%	3	4.7%	267	100%
3. Student interviews	24	37.5%	24	37.5%	3	4.7%	11	17.2%	2	3.1%	249	100%
4. Faculty interviews	26	40.6%	20	31.3%	2	3.1%	16	25.0%	0	0.0%	248	100%
5. Standard test scores	10	15.6%	14	21.9%	28	43.8%	6	9.4%	6	9.4%	208	100%
6. Teacher lesson plans	5	7.8%	27	42.2%	17	26.6%	9	14.1%	6	9.4%	208	100%
7. Librarian lesson plans	10	15.6%	22	34.4%	15	23.4%	0	0.0%	17	26.6%	200	100%
8. Library use reports	5	7.8%	24	37.5%	10	15.6%	9	14.1%	16	25.0%	185	100%
9. Nonteaching observation (formal)	0	0.0%	0	0.0%	9	14.1%	52	81.3%	3	4.7%	134	100%
10. Faculty surveys	1	1.6%	1	1.6%	3	4.7%	42	65.6%	17	26.6%	119	100%
11. Teaching observation (formal)	0	0.0%	1	1.6%	0	0.0%	55	85.9%	8	12.5%	122	100%
12. Budget reports	0	0.0%	0	0.0%	0	0.0%	42	65.6%	22	34.4%	106	100%
13. Circulation reports	0	0.0%	2	3.1%	3	4.7%	7	10.9%	52	81.3%	83	100%
14. Student surveys	0	0.0%	0	0.0%	4	6.3%	3	4.7%	57	89.1%	75	100%

N = 64

they are sensitive to issues of library climate. Further interviews revealed that principals looked for the following in their informal observations:

- Students are "actively engaged" with books or technology.
- The librarian is interacting with teachers and students.
- There is an organized, clean, inviting environment.
- A variety of materials are available.
- There are relevant displays.
- Students are borrowing books.

The Tulsa Model Librarian Evaluation and Observation Rubric (Tulsa Public Schools 2015) is very comprehensive and can serve as a guide. The document can be found at https://www.tulsaschools.org/about/teams /educator-effectiveness/tulsa-model.

EVALUATION OF THE SCHOOL LIBRARIAN IN INTERVIEWS

Being interviewed by school administrators may be the first time you are evaluated as a potential school librarian. There is a plethora of general resources available about succeeding in job interviews that offer sample questions and answers that will help you prepare and feel confident. One extensive list categorizes potential questions into the following areas (Doyle 2018):

- Questions about you
- Questions about leaving your previous job
- Qualifications
- Previous job performance
- Work history
- Management and teamwork
- Why you should be hired
- Questions about the company (school and/or district)
- Questions about your future
- Questions to ask them

More specific questions might include the following:

1. How would you build relationships with faculty?
2. How would you approach working with a difficult teacher?
3. How would you handle a parent's complaint about a resource?
4. How would you build relationships with students?
5. Do you consider yourself a leader? What motivates you to go the extra mile on projects?
6. How do you view the role of the librarian in state-mandated testing?

 7. How does working in a school library differ from being a classroom teacher?
 8. What is your experience in supervising library paraprofessionals?
 9. How would you manage the library's budget?
10. How would you reach reluctant readers?
11. How would you motivate underachievers?
12. How do you deal with discipline issues in the library?
13. How would you infuse technology into the curriculum?
14. How do you see the library program contributing to our mission and goals?
15. How would you encourage teachers to collaborate with you?
16. What background do you have with technology?
17. Why did you decide to become a school librarian?
18. What professional development have you participated in recently?
19. Describe the atmosphere you would like to create in the library.
20. What are some books that you would recommend to . . . (various audiences)?
21. If you were given the opportunity to design professional development for teachers, what would you like to do?
22. How would you get parents involved?
23. What aspect of being a librarian are you most passionate about?
24. What does collaboration mean to you?
25. Talk about some library programs you would like to initiate.

You might be asked to teach a lesson at the next phase of interviewing or prepare a lesson on the spot.

Things to Ask Them: Evaluating the Situation on the Fly

 1. Is there a school-wide information literacy curriculum?
 2. What technologies are students proficient with?
 3. How are students scheduled to come into the library? Is it a fixed schedule, flexible, or mixed?
 4. Can I have a tour of the library?
 5. What tech support is available for teachers?
 6. Is there clerical assistance? How many hours per week?
 7. Is the library closed for standardized testing? How many days?
 8. What is your vision for the school library?
 9. What professional development opportunities are available for faculty?
10. How does funding come to the library? Is the librarian expected to hold a bookfair?
11. What has been working well in the library that you would like to see continue?
12. What has not been working that you would not like to have continued?

SELF-EVALUATION

Leadership

For the past two decades, school librarians have been encouraged to take on leadership roles in their schools. "The American Association of School Librarians supports the position that full-time certified school librarians provide effective leadership in areas of curriculum development, instructional design, technology integration, professional development, student advocacy, information literacy instruction, and collaboration" (American Association of School Librarians 2018).

Recent research has analyzed major studies in the field to develop a theoretical basis that provides an informed understanding and explanation of the phenomenon of school librarian leadership (Everhart and Johnston 2016). Researchers identified key concepts and an explanation of their interdependence in a real-world context. This resulted in four fundamental propositions toward a theory of school librarian leadership, which can be seen in figure 2.4. School librarians can examine the model and propositions to assess conditions in their school culture and personal skill set that may encourage leadership growth or inhibit leadership. Table 2.2 illustrates how these propositions may present themselves in practice.

Figure 2.4 Conceptual Model of School Librarian Leadership

Source: Figure 2 (p19) in Everhart, Nancy, and Melissa P. Johnston. "A Proposed Theory of School Librarian Leadership: A Meta-Ethnographic Approach." *School Library Research* 19 (2016). Available online at http://www.ala.org/aasl/slr/volume19/everhartjohnston.

Table 2-2   Evidence of School Librarian Leadership

School Librarian Leadership Propositions	Evidence of Leadership
1. Education can provide a leadership skill set to bolster confidence for the growth of school librarian leadership.	• What do you draw upon from your college courses to make you feel confident as a school librarian? How have you adapted this content to your advantage?
2. Peers contribute to school librarian leadership growth.	• What is your professional learning network? What is missing that would help you become a leader? What can you do to help those new to the profession?
3. School librarian leadership growth requires a specific mind-set.	• Do you view yourself as a leader? Is there a critical incident that triggered this view?
4. School librarian leadership engagement follows traditional leadership patterns and is resistant to forms of leadership that require taking risks.	• How do you move beyond support and collaboration roles in becoming a transformational leader? How can you meet resistance in a positive manner to change people's minds?

Reflection

Reflection is an important component of school librarian self-evaluation. According to the National Board for Professional Teaching Standards (2012),

> Reflection is the purposeful, systematic self-examination of one's own practices and of developments in the library media field. Through reflection, accomplished library media specialists can extend their knowledge, improve student learning, advance and strengthen library media programs, and improve collaboration with other members of the learning community. Reflection is central to the responsibilities, professional growth, and leadership of the library media specialist.
>
> Accomplished library media specialists are committed to lifelong learning and understand that self-reflection is a continual process that strengthens their practice. Reflective about the learning process, specialists analyze how well their programs meet the needs of all students and determine how the library media program can be made rigorous, relevant, and effective. Specialists examine their own personal strengths and weaknesses, as well as those of the library media program, to improve professional practice. (51)

Reflection has been shown to have a positive relationship to problem-solving tendencies (Sivaci 2017), and library leaders use reflection as a problem-solving tool (Reale 2017). Several types of reflection have been defined that can be beneficial to school librarians (Jay and Johnson 2002, 77, Table 1).

Journals

Journals have historically been a reflective tool. Reale is an advocate of the traditional written journal and recommends purchasing "a journal that you will enjoy writing in. This is not as frivolous as it seems. Your thoughts and reflections are worthy of a bound journal that will be a pleasure to open" (2017, 67). She maintains that the physical act of writing down thoughts (rather than using a computer) promotes more crystallized thinking and that creating a ritual for writing, such as writing first thing in the morning or with a cup of tea at night, will make one feel comfortable and look forward to writing in the journal. A new type of journal, called a bullet journal, has gained popularity recently. Bullet journals are a combination of to-do lists, sketchbooks, notebooks, and diaries. This method encourages authors to examine how their goals, tasks, and responsibilities make them feel and is said to lead to more mindfulness and productivity.

Blogging

Blogs (weblogs) may be considered a form of digital journaling. Blogs are often used in preservice school librarian education as a way to have students reflect on their experiences and to begin to form professional identities (Miller and Williams 2013). Many find it useful to continue blogging as they enter the profession to gain valuable feedback and become part of the school librarian learning community. There are a variety of school librarians and school library thinkers who have large followings on their blogs (LaGarde 2018; Roche 2018; Jones 2018, Miller 2018; Valenza 2018).

Video Analysis

Video recording oneself teaching can be disconcerting, but it is also a valuable reflective exercise. When video is used in a manner that respects the professionalism of teachers, it can have a positive effect on teaching and learning because it provides a clear picture of reality and a way for measuring progress toward a goal (Knight 2014). For true self-reflection, you do not need to have someone else record you. Catapano (2018) recommends using a camera mounted on a tripod in the back of the room and establishing several areas to focus on:

- How loudly do I speak?
- Do I get off track at all? How often?
- Do I do anything annoying or distracting with my voice, gestures, posture, etc.?

- How clear are my instructions for activities?
- How clearly do I communicate the big ideas in a lesson?
- Am I interacting with students effectively?
- What are students doing as I am speaking?
- Does my method of instruction seem appropriate for the content and goal I have in mind?
- How much time do I spend talking about things that do not need to be talked about?

EXTERNAL EVALUATION

Peer Observation

Feedback from an evaluator lacking a school library background may not be as useful, or have the same impact, as that from a peer who understands the scope of your role (Zilonis and Swerling 2017). Solicit the help of a trusted colleague to observe you and your library program. The forms in this chapter could be used to formulate the observations and subsequent discussion of what is going well and what needs improvement.

National Board Certification

National Board Certification, a voluntary undertaking, is overseen by the National Board for Professional Teaching Standards. Achieving National Board Certification in Library Media has been considered the highest credential in the teaching profession, and fewer than 50 percent of those who attempt it are successful (Everhart and Dresang 2007).

One of thirty-five certification areas, Library Media, focuses on ten areas of accomplished practice:

Standard I: Knowledge of Students
Standard II: Teaching and Learning
Standard III: Knowledge of Library and Information Studies
Standard IV: Leadership
Standard V: Administration
Standard VI: Integration of Technologies
Standard VII: Access, Equity, and Diversity
Standard VIII: Ethics
Standard IX: Outreach and Advocacy
Standard X: Reflective Practice (National Board for Professional Teaching Standards 2018)

The rigorous certification process involves two parts: an assessment center section made up of content knowledge responses scored by computer and a portfolio section scored by trained assessors. The portfolio section contains three components: differentiation in instruction, teaching practice and learning environment, and an effective and reflective practitioner (National Board for Professional Teaching Standards 2012). Scores for National Board Certification are released once per year, and in some states and school districts, those who achieve are rewarded with pay raises (National Board for Professional Teaching Standards 2018). This high-level evaluation of professional knowledge and skills is recommended for those with at least three years' experience in the field.

EVALUATING CLERKS AND ASSISTANTS

Paraprofessional support personnel in school library centers are called library clerks, aides, paras, or assistants. For the purposes of discussion in this section, paid adult support staff will be referred to as *clerks* and student helpers as *aides*.

Interview Questions for a Library Clerk

If you are fortunate enough to have library clerical help, insist on being involved in the interview process. You are the one that will be working with the person hired on a daily basis. The interview will allow you to get a feel for the person and whether they come across as creative, flexible, and a self-starter. Melissa Davis (1997) gathered responses from LM_NET members on questions one should ask a library clerk in an interview. As each situation is different, you may want eliminate or add questions.

Work Experience and Work Ethic

- Tell us something about yourself and your experience, especially as it relates to working with children and adults.
- Tell us about your background, education, and work experiences that qualify you for this job.
- Please describe your training and work experience.
- Why are you applying for this job?
- Why do you feel you are the right person for this job?
- Describe your work philosophy.
- Describe a "typical" day in your current work environment. What responsibilities are you entrusted with?
- What do you believe is the most important job of the library clerk?
- Are you willing to ask questions if you do not understand how to do something?
- How many personal calls do you receive during the day?

- How would you handle a teacher or acquaintance who comes into the library and wants to chat for more than a minute or two?
- What do you do when you have finished all your tasks?

Organizational Abilities

- What process do you use to plan and organize your day, and how do you react to unexpected changes in your planned schedule?
- You will often have several tasks to do. How would you determine the order in which to do them?

Physical

- Can you stoop, bend, reach, and lift easily? This job involves shelving and getting materials from bookshelves at floor level as well as at waist and shoulder height. Will this be a problem for you?

Creativity

- Describe a project that you have completed that used your creativity.

Technical/Computer

- Describe your experience using computers or other equipment.
- What is the last new piece of hardware or software you learned? When was that, and how did you go about learning it?
- As the library is fully automated, tell us about any experiences you have had with library automation systems and also about your computer experiences in general.
- Are you willing to learn new equipment?

Readers

- Tell us about some of your favorite authors and outstanding literature for students of this age.
- Have you been a library volunteer?
- A student wants to check out a book on a topic you loathe. What do you do?
- What do you know about student privacy related to the library?
- If a student comes in and wants a book that is checked out to another student, what would you do?
- Do you think there are any books students should not be reading?
- Tell me about a favorite book of yours.
- What are you reading now (or have just finished recently)?

Discipline

- The librarian is not there when an angry parent comes in and demands that a book be removed or will not pay a fine no matter what the records show. What do you do?
- What is the most important thing to remember when you are disciplining a child?
- Do you really like/get along with kids this age?
- Can you handle discipline so that I do not have to rescue you?
- How would you handle a student who came into the library with an open soda can and did not want to leave?

Closing

- Is there something else you think we should know about you?
- Do you have any questions for us?

SCHOOL LIBRARIAN EVALUATION OF THE LIBRARY CLERK

In some schools, even though clerks work under the supervision of the school librarian, they get evaluated by school administrators. In others, the school librarian may do the evaluation using a standard required clerical form that may not cover the multitudinous tasks performed in the school library. You may seek permission to design an add-on evaluation form similar to the one here (see table 2.3) or use elements of it to devise a unique one.

Table 2-3   School Library Clerk Evaluation Form

Collection

Conducts inventory	Excellent	Very Good	Average	Fair	Needs Improvement
Shelves materials	Excellent	Very Good	Average	Fair	Needs Improvement
Reads and straightens shelves	Excellent	Very Good	Average	Fair	Needs Improvement
Mends materials	Excellent	Very Good	Average	Fair	Needs Improvement
Updates newspapers and magazines	Excellent	Very Good	Average	Fair	Needs Improvement

Circulation

Checks in materials	Excellent	Very Good	Average	Fair	Needs Improvement
Checks out materials	Excellent	Very Good	Average	Fair	Needs Improvement
Maintains notices	Excellent	Very Good	Average	Fair	Needs Improvement

Continued

Table 2-3   Continued

Organization

Keeps media center neat and orderly	Excellent	Very Good	Average	Fair	Needs Improvement
Maintains records	Excellent	Very Good	Average	Fair	Needs Improvement
Completes requested reports	Excellent	Very Good	Average	Fair	Needs Improvement

Acquisition

Processes materials	Excellent	Very Good	Average	Fair	Needs Improvement
Verifies bibliographic data	Excellent	Very Good	Average	Fair	Needs Improvement
Keeps supplies available and ordered	Excellent	Very Good	Average	Fair	Needs Improvement

Public Relations

Assists teachers	Excellent	Very Good	Average	Fair	Needs Improvement
Assists students	Excellent	Very Good	Average	Fair	Needs Improvement
Produces bulletin boards/ displays	Excellent	Very Good	Average	Fair	Needs Improvement
Coordinates special events	Excellent	Very Good	Average	Fair	Needs Improvement
Liaison with volunteers	Excellent	Very Good	Average	Fair	Needs Improvement
Assists with correspondence	Excellent	Very Good	Average	Fair	Needs Improvement

Technical

Data entry/database maintenance	Excellent	Very Good	Average	Fair	Needs Improvement
Maintains equipment	Excellent	Very Good	Average	Fair	Needs Improvement
Assists with makerspaces	Excellent	Very Good	Average	Fair	Needs Improvement

After the formal evaluation is conducted by either the school librarian or administration, it is a good idea to also sit down for an informal discussion with the clerk. If you have more than one clerk, meet with each one individually. Schedule a time when you will not be interrupted. The goal of the conversation should be to review strategies for improvement for the next year. As a starting point, here are some sample questions to stimulate dialogue:

1. What do you feel you accomplished this year?
2. What do you need more time for?

3. Do you see any areas where we can streamline operations?
4. My major goal(s) for next year is/are______. How do you think you can help?
5. What is/are your major goal(s) for next year? How can I help?
6. Do you need more training in any particular area? How can I help?
7. What areas of the library program do you think need improvement? Why? Do you have any ideas on how to achieve this?
8. What can I do to help you do a better job?

You may want to give the list of questions to the clerk a day or so before your planned meeting. That way, the person will have time to ponder the questions and their possible responses.

STUDENT AIDES

Many school librarians at all levels use student aides in lieu of support or paid help. An application or interview process will help establish those that are sincerely interested from those that are not. Typical applications require the following:

- Name, grade, and teacher
- Parent's signature of consent
- List of free times to work
- Two or more teacher signatures/recommendations

An application may also have questions requiring written responses:

1. Why do you want to become a library student assistant?
2. Do you feel that you are responsible and capable of being a library student assistant?
3. What is your knowledge of computers/technology? Are you willing to learn?
4. Do you have good organizational skills? Are you interested in learning?
5. Do you like to read?
6. Do you like to help other students?
7. Do you like to help teachers?
8. What do you like to do when you are in the library?
9. Are you a hard worker, and are you willing to work at a high energy level?
10. Do you like to research?
11. Do you like to shelve books and keep them in order?

For younger children, they may be asked to write a simple paragraph explaining why they want to be a library aide, or they may simply be asked.

Some school librarians have also devised simple tests, such as shelving books or alphabetizing.

Library Aide Evaluation

"Student assistant programs are dynamic. Change is the ever-present constant, but evaluation can help you identify aspects of the program that have a degree of consistency. You can use these as a core around which to revise and modify your program" (Bard 1999, 122). There are a variety of methods that can be used alone or in combination to evaluate student assistants (Bard 1999):

1. *Direct observation*—Observe and correct errors and suggest more efficient ways of doing a library task in a way that encourages learning and enhances self-esteem.
2. *Logs and portfolios*—Student provides examples and visual documentation of his or her best work.
3. *Student self-evaluation*—Student writes freely on a topic or series of questions. Some examples include the following:

   - What are the best things about being a library aide?
   - What are the worst things about being a library aide?
   - Name three things you learned while working in the library.
   - Is there anything you would have liked to learn but did not?
   - What advice would you give to new library aides?
   - Do you have any other comments?

4. *Contribution to the library program*—Keep pre- and post-data about program aspects such as the following:

   - Has the library benefited from the students' having returned books and other items to their correct location promptly?
   - Is the facility more attractive and inviting without materials stacked here and there waiting to be put away?
   - Is the circulation increasing because materials are readily accessible?
   - Are you able to spend more time on professional activities and planning because this nonprofessional task is being done to your expectation?

5. *Staff evaluation*—Staff evaluate students when they are performing tasks while the librarian is not present.
6. *Faculty evaluation*—Teachers evaluate the helpfulness of student aides and the value of their work to them and their students via open-ended questions or a short survey.

REFERENCES

American Association of School Librarians. 2018. "The Strategic Leadership Role of School Librarians." http://www.ala.org/aasl/sites/ala.org.aasl/files/content/aaslissues/positionstatements/AASL_Position%20Statement_Strategic%20Leadership%20Role_2018-06-24.pdf.

Bard, Therese Bissen. 1999. *Student Assistants in the School Library Media Center*. Englewood, CO: Libraries Unlimited.

Catapano, Jordan. 2018. "A Technique for Self-Reflection: Video Recording." TeachHub. https://www.teachhub.com/teaching-strategies/2014/10/teaching-strategies-the-value-of-self-reflection/.

Danielson Group. 2018. "A Vision of Excellence." https://danielsongroup.org/framework.

Davis, Melissa. 1997. "Questions to Ask Aide Applicants." LM_NET, Last modified May 29. http://lmnet-archive.iis.syr.edu/LM_NET-pre2000/1997/May_1997/msg01690.html.

Doyle, Alison. 2018. "Job Interview Questions and Best Answers." *The Balance*, April 13. https://www.thebalance.com/job-interview-questions-and-answers-2061204.

Elkins, Aaron J. 2014. "What's Expected, What's Required, and What's Measured: A Comparative Qualitative Content Analysis of the National Professional Standards for School Librarians, and Their Job Descriptions and Performance Evaluations in Florida." PhD diss., Florida State University. http://purl.flvc.org/fsu/fd/FSU_migr_etd-8978.

Everhart, Nancy. 2006. "Principals' Evaluation of School Librarians: A Study of Strategic and Nonstrategic Evidence-Based Approaches." *School Libraries Worldwide* 12 (2): 38–51. https://iasl-online.org/Resources/Documents/slw/v12/12_2everhart.pdf.

Everhart, Nancy, and Eliza T. Dresang. 2007. "Integrating Research Results and National Board Certification Standards into a Leadership Curriculum for School Library Media Specialists." *Journal of Education for Library and Information Science* 48 (4): 272–83. https://www.jstor.org/stable/40323793.

Everhart, Nancy, and Melissa P. Johnston. 2016. "A Proposed Theory of School Librarian Leadership: A Meta-Ethnographic Approach." *School Library Research* 19: 1–30. ERIC (EJ1120868).

Jay, Joelle K., and Kerri L. Johnson. 2002. "Capturing Complexity: A Typology of Reflective Practice for Teacher Education." *Teaching and Teacher Education* 18 (1): 73–85. doi:10.1016/S0742-051X(01)00051-8.

Jones, Gwyneth A. 2018. *The Daring Librarian* (blog). https://www.thedaringlibrarian.com.

Knight, Jim. 2014. "What You Learn When You See Yourself Teach." *Educational Leadership* 71 (8): 18–23. ERIC (EJ1043761).

LaGarde, Jennifer. 2018. *The Adventures of Library Girl* (blog). https://www.librarygirl.net.

Miller, Shannon McClintock. 2018. *The Library Voice* (blog). https://vanmeterlibraryvoice.blogspot.com.

Miller, Wendy, and Rachel Marie-Crane Williams. 2013. "Preservice Teachers and Blogs: An Invitation to Extended Reflection and Conversation." *Art Education* 66 (3): 47–52. ERIC (EJ1041062).

Moreillon, Judi. 2013. "Educating for School Library Leadership: Developing the Instructional Partnership Role." *Journal of Education for Library and Information Science* 54 (1): 55–66. ERIC (EJ1074121).

National Board for Professional Teaching Standards. 2012. *Library Media Standards*. n.p.: National Board for Professional Teaching Standards. http://accomplishedteacher.org/wp-content/uploads/2017/02/ECYA-LM.pdf.

National Board for Professional Teaching Standards. 2018. "What Teachers Should Know and Be Able to Do." http://accomplishedteacher.org.

National Center for Education Statistics. 2012. "Schools and Staffing Survey (SASS)." https://nces.ed.gov/surveys/sass/tables_list.asp#2012.

Pennsylvania Department of Education. 2013. "Possible Guiding Questions: Conversations between Principals and Teachers." Last modified June 20. http://static.pdesas.org/content/documents/Guiding%20Questions%20For%20School%20Librarians%206-20-2013.pdf.

Reale, Michelle. 2017. *Becoming a Reflective Librarian and Teacher: Strategies for Mindful Academic Practice*. Chicago: ALA Editions.

Roche, Caroline. 2018. *Heart of the School* (blog). http://heartoftheschool.edublogs.org.

Sivaci, Sadik Yüksel. 2017. "The Relationship between Reflective Thinking Tendencies and Social Problem Solving Abilities of Pre-Service Teachers." *Journal of Education and Training Studies* 5 (11): 21–31. ERIC (EJ1157842).

Tulsa Public Schools. 2015. "Tulsa Model for Observation and Evaluation: Librarian." https://www.tulsaschools.org/about/teams/educator-effectiveness/tulsa-model.

Valenza, Joyce. 2018. *NeverEnding Search* (blog). *School Library Journal.* http://blogs.slj.com/neverendingsearch.

Zilonis, Mary Frances, and Chris Swerling. 2017. "Meaningful Feedback." *School Library Connection*, August/September (1): 25.

Chapter 3

Collections

"The collection is at the center of the school library, and expert curation, conducted by a qualified school librarian, is essential to ensuring that the collection meets the needs of learners and educators" (American Association of School Librarians 2018, 98). The collection is also the most evaluated of the entire program because is very tangible and visible. It is easy to collect data on the overall size of the collection as well as its component parts, for example, Dewey classes, picture books, periodicals, videos, e-books, and the like. It also is relatively straightforward to obtain budget information about how much money has been spent in each of these sections and to make simple calculations as to number of items per student and amount of money spent per student for library materials. A simple count may be all that is needed for this type of quantitative evaluation.

In qualitative evaluation, the school librarian addresses the quality of what is available to users, or what constitutes a good collection. Rather than providing simple collection counts and dollar figures, qualitative evaluation yields data about how the collection meets user needs. Some qualitative evaluation techniques include (1) checking lists, catalogs, and bibliographies; (2) direct examination; (3) obtaining user opinions; (4) applying standards; and (5) compiling comparative statistics (Mardis 2016).

Intner and Futas (1994) discuss the problems that may be uncovered by an evaluation of the collection:

- Mismatches between currently held collections and the people they are supposed to serve.
- Peculiarities in placement of materials that cause problems for browsers. These peculiarities do not bother librarians; they are so used to dealing with these quirks that they no longer see them.
- Differences in the way individual librarians budget, allocate, select, or weed.
- Gaps in the existing written documentation for collection policies and procedures.

Once the data is collected, decisions need to be made regarding further collection development. Four factors will affect these decisions: background of the users (age, ethnic group, languages spoken), material use (what circulated well in the immediate past is likely to circulate well in the future, and what did not probably won't), shelf allocations (how space is divided among the various classifications and formats), and user views of individual items on the shelf (unpleasant-looking or worn materials are candidates for weeding; moving materials around that are above or below eye level will be beneficial to their circulation) (Intner and Futas 1994).

EVALUATING MATERIALS TO BE ADDED TO THE COLLECTION—SELECTION

School Library Selection Criteria

The American Library Association (2018) maintains that criteria for the selection of materials are dependent on the goals and objectives of the educational institution of which the library is a part; however, there are general criteria that will fit most, if not all, school libraries.

General Criteria:

- Support and enrich the curriculum and/or students' personal interests and learning
- Meet high standards in literary, artistic, and aesthetic quality; technical aspects; and physical format
- Be appropriate for the subject area and for the age, emotional development, ability level, learning styles, and social, emotional, and intellectual development of the students for whom the materials are selected
- Incorporate accurate and authentic factual content from authoritative sources
- Earn favorable reviews in standard reviewing sources and/or favorable recommendations based on preview and examination of materials by professional personnel

- Exhibit a high degree of potential user appeal and interest
- Represent differing viewpoints on controversial issues
- Provide a global perspective and promote diversity by including materials by authors and illustrators of all cultures
- Include a variety of resources in physical and virtual formats including print and non-print such as electronic and multimedia (including subscription databases and other online products, eBooks, educational games, and other forms of emerging technologies)
- Demonstrate physical format, appearance, and durability suitable to their intended use
- Balance cost with need

Top Five Recommended School Library Reviewing Sources:

- Association for Library Service to Children (ALSC) Notable Children's Books
- Booklist
- School Library Journal
- We Need Diverse Books website
- Young Adult Library Services Association (YALSA)

Evaluating Jobbers of Library Materials

Library jobbers are a convenient way to order materials from multiple publishers at once at a discount. They also have processing services so that when the materials arrive one only needs to perform minimal tasks, such as downloading MARC records and stamping identification information before they are shelf-ready. In the list that follows, all except Amazon and Barnes & Noble (which can be used for "rush" orders of popular books) are jobbers frequently employed in school libraries.

- Amazon
- Baker & Taylor
- Barnes & Noble
- Bound to Stay Bound Books
- Brodart
- Follett Library Resources
- Ingram Library Services, Inc.
- Mackin
- Perma-Bound

Because there are several choices for jobbers, each with slightly different options, some factors you might want use for comparison are found in table 3.1. Check off services that are important, and cross out those that are not needed. Tally the columns and consider using the vendor with the most checks.

Table 3-1   Evaluating Jobbers

Jobber	1.	2.	3.	4.
Ordering				
Typing service				
Free collection analysis				
Budgeting (do not exceed)				
Books and other materials (audiovisual, e-books)				
Wish lists (for teachers, students, parents)				
Free shipping				
Library bindings				
Foreign language materials				
Processing				
MARC records				
Theft detection				
Date due slip/pocket				
Classification by genre or call numbers				
Spine labels				
Mylar book cover				
Bar code labels				
School property labels				
RFID tags				
Reading Counts/Accelerated Reader services				
Other				
Local rep				
Replacement guarantee				
Average cost of a sample of ten titles				
Turnaround time from order to receipt				

QUANTITATIVE EVALUATION OF THE COLLECTION

Evaluation of the Collection Based on Holdings

Automated library management systems provide reports of the total number of items in a collection as well as other statistics. Some might also calculate the percentages of the collection in each class or category. The total library holdings can now be used as a basis of comparison to a variety of standards, both state and national. Table 3.2 shows recommendations from the state of Mississippi.

Table 3-2 Balanced Dewey Recommendations for the School Library Collection

	Elementary (Pre-K–5)	Middle (6–8)	High (9–12)
000 Generalities	0.5%	1%	1%
100 Philosophy and Psychology	0.5%	1%	1%
200 Religion	1%	1%	1%
300 Social Sciences	8%	10%	11%
400 Language	1%	1%	1%
500 Science/Mathematics	11%	9%	7%
600 Technology	5%	7%	6%
700 The Arts	4%	5%	6%
800 Literature	4%	5%	10%
900 Geography and History	7%	13%	11%
General Fiction	23%	26%	15%
Reference	3%	9%	18%
Biography	6%	10%	9%
Professional	2%	1%	2%
Story Collection	0%	1%	1%
Easy	23%	0%	0%

Source: "Mississippi Public and Nonpublic School Library Guide and Resources," Mississippi Department of Education, 2017, p. 46.

Collection guidelines have more recently focused on qualitative approaches. For example, Texas recommends "a balanced, carefully selected, and systematically organized collection of print and electronic library resources that are sufficient to meet students' needs in all subject areas and that are continuously monitored for currency and relevancy" (Texas State Library and Archives Commission 2017, 5).

Evaluation of the Collection by Comparing Expenditures

Data on average expenditures and costs are meaningful to school librarians as they propose budgets to their administrators. Having statistics on other schools can boost confidence when requesting reasonable funding for library collections and may also compel principals to increase allotments if you fall "below average."

If you use the figures on recommended collection size previously posted, you can begin to calculate a budget based on recent prices of library editions of books shown in figure 3.1 (*School Library Journal* 2019).

An ongoing report of expenditures in school libraries appears every few years in the *School Library Journal*. Data on collections is presented in

Children's Titles

Fiction Hardcover	$17.95
Non-fiction Library Binding	$26.72

Young Adult Titles

Fiction Hardcover	$18.95
Non-fiction hardcover	$37.68

Adult Titles

Fiction Hardcover	$25.95
Non-fiction Hardcover*	$28.67
Graphic Novels	$20.80

*excludes reference books

Figure 3.1 Average book prices, 2019

Source: Adatped from "SLJ's Average Book Prices for 2019." School Library Journal, March 11. https://www.slj.com/?detailStory=slj-average-book-prices-2019.

Table 3-3 Average Materials Expenditures for 2016–2017 in U.S. School Libraries

	Average Expenditures	**Your Expenditures**
Total budget	$6,907	
Budget per student	$12.45	
Print books	$5,210	
Periodicals	$493	
Databases	$3,652	
E-books	$1,021	
DVDs/Blu-rays	$332	
Streaming media	$1,712	

Source: School Library Journal Research, 2018.

table 3.3 for the school year 2016–2017 and was collected from a nation-wide sample (*School Library Journal* 2019). It can be used to compare to your local situation.

EVALUATING ITEMS TO REMOVE FROM THE COLLECTION—WEEDING

Some of the same principles used in selecting materials can also be applied to weeding (deselecting) the collection. The Texas State Library and Archives Commission (2012) provides general guidance as well as specific criteria for the Dewey classes.

For all items, consider the following problem categories and related issues:

Poor Content

- Outdated and obsolete information (especially on subjects that change quickly or require absolute currency, such as computers, law, science, space, health and medicine, technology, travel)
- Trivial subject matter, including topics that are no longer of interest or that were dealt with superficially due to their popularity at a specific point in time, as well as titles related to outdated popular culture
- Mediocre writing style, especially material that was written quickly to meet popular interest that has passed
- Inaccurate or false information, including outdated information and sources that have been superseded by new titles or editions
- Unused sets of books (although you may keep specific volumes if they meet local needs and are used)
- Repetitious series, especially series that are no longer popular or that were published to meet a popular demand that no longer exists
- Superseded editions (in general, it is unnecessary to keep more than one previous edition, discarding as new editions are added)
- Resources that are not on standard lists or that were never reviewed in standard review sources
- Material that contains biased, racist, or sexist terminology or views
- Unneeded duplicates, especially if they are worn or tattered
- Self-published or small press materials that are not circulating, especially if they were added as gifts

Materials/Books of Poor Appearance

- Worn out, ragged items
- Poorly bound or poorly printed editions

- Rebound editions that are worn and shabby or have torn pages
- Items that are dirty, shabby, warped, bug infested, or otherwise marked up, mutilated, or "edited" by patrons
- Books with very small print or poor-quality pictures
- Scratched CDs or DVDs, brittle film or magnetic tape (in the case of video and audiocassettes); equipment no longer available to play
- Media that is beaten up from wear or has broken or missing parts
- Books with yellowed, brittle, torn, taped, or missing pages
- Books with dust jackets or cover art that is dated, especially on children's and young adult books

Unused Materials

- Items that have not circulated within the past three to five years and have not been used for reference or in-house research
- Duplicate copies that are no longer needed, regardless of condition
- Periodicals that are not indexed
- Periodicals that are available in full-text databases
- Unused volumes in sets or series
- Unneeded titles in subject areas that are less frequently used
- Materials on the "hot topics" that were popular more than five years ago
- More books than are needed on any single subject
- Formats that are no longer popular in your community, especially if the technology needed to use the format is no longer owned by people in the community
- Material that is no longer important to the collection because of changes in local demographics, school curricula, or other factors

Checklist of Weeding Factors

For all materials, consider the following:

- *Date*—When was the item published? When was it added to the collection?
- *Author*—Is the author still read or likely to be read in the future? Is the book a lesser work?
- *Publisher*—Was the book self-published or published by an "instant" press that may not have taken care in editing and printing?
- *Physical condition*—Are there any factors that make the item unattractive?
- *Additional copies*—Are more copies available that may be in better condition?

- *Other books on the same subject in the collection*—If this book is discarded, what else is available?
- *Expense of replacement*—Can the item be replaced? Was this an expensive item that might benefit from rebinding or refurbishing rather than replacement?
- *Shelf time*—How long has the item sat on the shelf without circulating?
- *Relevance of the subject to the community*—Is the material of interest to anyone in the school community?

For juvenile and young adult materials, also consider the following:

- *Format*—Paperbacks are preferred by many young adults; board books get a lot of wear in tiny hands.
- *Reading level*—Is the level too high or too easy for young patrons who would be interested in the item?
- *Current interest in the subject matter*—Are young people interested in the subject? Is the treatment of the subject engaging?
- *Visual appeal*—Are the illustrations in color? Are photographs clear? Is the layout of the book open (white space) and inviting?
- *Jacket art (contemporary versus outmoded)*—Does the book look like something your great-grandmother read?
- *Use in school curricula*—Are books available for the grade level where the subject is studied? Are teachers assigning specific titles?

Automated library systems can save valuable time by performing collection analyses that make recommendations for weeding. Figure 3.2 shows a sample report from Mackin Educational Resources (2018) for titles that should be considered for weeding in one school. Using this system, school librarians can easily fill in the gaps by ordering new recommended titles to replace the weeded ones. Follett School Solutions's (2019) Titlewave is a similar product.

QUALITATIVE EVALUATION OF THE COLLECTION

As students continue to increase their use of electronic sources, quantitative evaluation of the collection will decrease. It will ultimately be more important to evaluate how well the collection meets particular curricular needs than to calculate how many items reside on the shelves in a particular subject. Rather than keeping items "just in case" they might be needed, it is more cost-effective to have access to materials "just in time."

Older Titles to consider for Weeding

Dewey	Title	MainEntry	Date	BarCode
342.73 DE	Becoming a citizen	De Capua, Sarah	2002	T 55824
342.73 WE	We the kids : the preamble to the Constitution of the United		2002	T 19503
345.744 WOO	Salem witchcraft trials : a headline court case	Woods, Geraldine	2000	T 70377
347.73 HEA	Supreme Court of the United States	Heath, David	1999	T 46681
355 SIE	U.S. Army at war	Sievert, Terri	2002	T 55696
356.16 CLA	Airborne : a guided tour of an airborne task force	Clancy, Tom	1997	T 65960
356.16 CLA	Special forces : a guided tour of U.S. Army Special Forces	Clancy, Tom	2001	T 66023
358.4 GRE	United States Air Force	Green, Michael	1998	T 46731
358.4 HOL	Air Force aircraft	Holden, Henry M	2001	T 46838
359 ABR	U.S. Navy at war	Abramovitz, Melissa	2002	T 55697
359.3 COO	U.S.S. Constitution	Cooper, Jason	2001	T 46733
359.9 BUR	Nuclear submarines	Burgan, Michael	2001	T 46524
359.9 BUR	Supercarriers	Burgan, Michael	2001	T 46680
359.9 BUR	U.S. Navy special forces : SEAL teams	Burgan, Michael	2000	T 55707
359.9 STR	U.S. Navy SEALs	Streissguth, Thomas	1996	T 46732
359.94 CLA	Carrier : a guided tour of an aircraft carrier	Clancy, Tom	1999	T 65971
359.96 CLA	Marine : a guided tour of a Marine expeditionary unit	Clancy, Tom	1996	T 65996
362.1 VIE	Views from our shoes : growing up with a brother or sister w		1997	T 29393
362.1 VIE	Views from our shoes : growing up with a brother or sister w		1997	T 70080
362.29 COB	Speed and your brain : the incredibly disgusting story	Cobb, Allan B	2000	T 29294
362.292 HYD	Alcohol 101 : an overview for teens	Hyde, Margaret O	1999	T 64000
362.4 LAK	Helen Keller and the big storm	Lakin, Patricia	2002	T 73683
362.4 ONE	Being blind	O'Neill, Linda	2000	T 45558
362.4 ONE	Being paralyzed	O'Neill, Linda	2000	T 45559
362.4 SCH	Some kids use wheelchairs	Schaefer, Lola M	2001	T 46653
362.7 PET	I have a sister, my sister is deaf	Peterson, Jeanne Whitel	1977	T 31701
362.7 PET	I have a sister, my sister is deaf	Peterson, Jeanne Whitel	1977	T 13768
362.76 PEL	man named Dave : a story of triumph and forgiveness	Pelzer, David J	2000	T 48784
363.1 BAL	Exploring the Titanic	Ballard, Robert D	1988	T 28978
363.1 FEL	My school bus : a book about school bus safety	Feldman, Heather	2000	T 46496
363.1 FEL	My school bus : a book about school bus safety	Feldman, Heather	2000	T 46495
363.12 BRE	Challenger disaster : tragic space flight	Bredeson, Carmen	1999	T 46106
363.2 GEO	Bomb detection dogs	George, Charles	1998	T 55107
363.2 KOT	day with police officers	Kottke, Jan	2000	T 80759
363.3 KAL	Floods	Kalz, Jill	2002	T 55283
363.34 SHE	Hurricane Andrew : nature's rage	Sherrow, Victoria	1998	T 46318
363.34 SHE	Plains outbreak tornadoes : killer twisters	Sherrow, Victoria	1998	T 46566
363.6 BUR	day in the life of a park ranger	Burby, Liza N	1999	T 46549
363.7 BAN	Common ground : the water, earth, and air we share	Bang, Molly	1997	T 45245
363.7 FRO	Keeping water clean	Frost, Helen	1999	T 55427
363.7 FRO	Keeping water clean	Frost, Helen	1999	T 47080
363.7 HAM	Eco-disasters	Hamilton, John	1993	T 46192
363.73 DUD	Oil spills! : the perils of petroleum	Duden, Jane	1999	T 40728
364.1 BER	All the President's men	Bernstein, Carl	1994	T 31161
364.1 PLA	Pirate	Platt, Richard	1994	T 31496
364.1 SHE	World Trade Center bombing : terror in the towers	Sherrow, Victoria	1998	T 47172
364.1 STE	Gangs	Stewart, Gail	2002	T 55302
364.15 CAP	In cold blood : a true account of a multiple murder and its	Capote, Truman	1994	T 70716
364.16 LAN	100 things you should know about pirates.	Langley, Andrew	2001	T 49015
364.16 SHE	Oklahoma City bombing : terror in the heartland	Sherrow, Victoria	1998	T 47104
365 CLI	Correction officer	Clinton, Susan	1998	T 46151
370 FEL	Don't whistle in school : the history of America's public sc	Feldman, Ruth Tenzer	2001	T 55928
370 GRA	Going to school during the Civil War : the Confederacy	Graves, Kerry A	2002	T 55979
370 GRA	Going to school during the Civil War : the Union	Graves, Kerry A	2002	T 55978
370 GRA	Going to school in pioneer times	Graves, Kerry A	2002	T 55982
370 SAT	Going to school in Colonial America	Sateren, Shelley Swanso	2002	T 55981
370 WEB	School in grandma's day	Weber, Valerie	1999	T 56140
370 WIL	day in the life of a Colonial schoolteacher	Wilmore, Kathy	2000	T 55913
370 WIL	day in the life of a Colonial schoolteacher	Wilmore, Kathy	2000	T 46163

Figure 3.2 Mackin report: Older titles to consider for weeding

Mackin.com

Matching the Collection to the Users

The best school library collections support the needs of their users. For this support to occur, background knowledge is required about various user characteristics. Data should be collected that will supply these characteristics. School librarians needing help in determining what types of data to collect and where to find it will be aided by these criteria and explanations, which were provided by the Maryland State Department of Education (1987, 92–97) and are still relevant today.

Ability and Achievement Levels

- What are the ability levels (cognitive, affective, and psychomotor) of students in each class and grade? How do the levels at which students are operating related to the course content and general methods of instruction employed in each class and grade? What materials would match or fulfill the needs of students in each class or grade?

- What are the achievement levels of students in each class and grade compared to their ability levels? What does the comparison reflect in terms of course content and method of instruction? What materials would contribute to student learning if there is significant disparity at either end of the spectrum? What materials would contribute to student learning where there is low achievement and high ability, or high ability and high achievement, etc.?

- What are the reading levels of students in each class and grade? How does the overall reading level affect course content and method of instruction? What is the range in readability of materials needed in each course, subject area, and grade to support the reading level of these students?

- How are students of different ability levels grouped for instruction in each class or grade? How does this grouping relate to the course content and methods of instruction in each class and grade? What effect does this grouping have on materials that might be effective with entire classes, small groups, or individuals?

- Is the creativity level of students promoted by the majority of staff? What materials have been selected or provided to encourage fluency, flexibility, and elaboration in creative and critical thinking?

- What is the general emotional wellbeing of students in each class and grade? How does this affect course content and methods of instruction? What materials are available to support students with special problems?

- What is the range of physical differences of students in each class and grade? How have these differences affected course content and methods of instruction? What special material and equipment must be provided for some students?

Learning Modes

- What is known about the learning modes of students in each class and grade? How has instruction been designed to capitalize on students' strengths in learning through sight, sound, touch, etc.? What audiovisual and other nonprint materials are needed in each content or subject area? What formats might be more productive in facilitating learning?
- How has the grouping of students with different learning modality strengths affected content and methods of instruction? What nonprint formats and accompanying equipment would support instruction of these students?

Learning Styles

- What is known about the learning or cognitive styles of students in each class and grade? How have these styles affected the content and method of instruction in each class and grade? What materials are needed to both challenge students and to support their learning styles?
- How has the grouping of students with different learning styles affected content and methods of instruction? What materials and equipment might be necessary in each content or subject area to more appropriately support student interaction and learning?

Ethnic and Cultural Background

- What is the ethnic and cultural background of each student in every class and grade? Does the collection include materials that supportively reflect those ethnic and cultural differences in each subject or content area?

Language Differences

- What are the speech and language differences of students in each class? What are some of the languages read or spoken by bilingual students? How have language differences affected the course content or subject area in each class and grade? What materials might be useful in each content or subject area that would help students with language differences learn?

Maturity Levels

- How is the maturity or sophistication level of students reflected in acquisitions to the collection? What materials might be helpful in certain areas of the curriculum?

Interest Levels

- What are some of the more prevalent interests of students in each class and grade? Do these interests relate to areas of the curriculum? What materials have been acquired that reflect these interests? What materials and equipment are necessary to make the collection more responsive to the interests of students?

Methods for Collecting Student Data

Information about the people served by the school library may be gathered in a variety of ways. In fact, all of the strategies may be used together for a better review of the collection. This data collection process is continuous for library staff who wish to predict and purchase those resources of greatest instructional value. Several strategies are valid for learning about items that will contribute to a more viable collection.

Review of Student Records

Cumulative student records and reports furnish achievement data, school progress data, attendance figures, health information, and other anecdotal records. Sample work, reading scores on various tests, and even interest inventories are often part of the students' files. When examining records of various faculty's classes, the school librarian learns more about ability levels and the kinds of materials that would be beneficial for instruction.

Conversations with Students

Informal discussions with students about their interests and concerns offer valuable insights that are especially advantageous when searching for materials that will motivate them. Students will reveal areas of personal interest and may comment about curriculum areas where more information is needed. Discussion and active listening can be powerful, effective methods for gaining information.

Conducting Surveys

One of the best techniques to determine how well your collection is meeting the needs of users is to ask them. A survey for students is shown in table 3.4 and one for faculty directly follows in table 3.5. When collection satisfaction surveys are repeated over time, usually two or three times a year, it is possible to compare satisfaction rates to determine whether the collection is getting better or worse at meeting patron expectations. Feedback also allows the librarian to know what areas need work (North Texas Regional Library System 2018).

Table 3-4   Student Opinion of the Library Collection Survey

Rate the Library Collection in the Following Areas:	Excellent	Good	Fair	Poor
Nonfiction books	4	3	2	1
Fiction books	4	3	2	1
Paperbacks	4	3	2	1
Audiobooks	4	3	2	1
E-books	4	3	2	1
Newspapers	4	3	2	1
Magazines	4	3	2	1
Internet resources	4	3	2	1
Databases	4	3	2	1
Computers and printers	4	3	2	1
Digital equipment	4	3	2	1
Computer software	4	3	2	1
Maker materials	4	3	2	1
Materials for school assignments	4	3	2	1
Materials for personal interests	4	3	2	1

Indicate Your Level of Agreement with the Following Statements:

It is easy to locate materials in the library.	Strongly agree	Agree	Disagree	Strongly disagree
The library collection is up-to-date.	Strongly agree	Agree	Disagree	Strongly disagree
The library collection is attractive.	Strongly agree	Agree	Disagree	Strongly disagree
The materials in the library collection are interesting.	Strongly agree	Agree	Disagree	Strongly disagree
There are enough materials in the library.	Strongly agree	Agree	Disagree	Strongly disagree

I Would Like to See More Books about the Following:

____

____

What Improvements in Access to Information Would You Find Most Useful?

____

____

____

Table 3-5   Faculty Opinion of the Library Collection Survey

Rate the Library Collection in the Following Areas:	**Excellent**	**Good**	**Fair**	**Poor**
Nonfiction books	4	3	2	1
Fiction books	4	3	2	1
Paperbacks	4	3	2	1
Audiobooks	4	3	2	1
E-books	4	3	2	1
Newspapers	4	3	2	1
Magazines	4	3	2	1
Internet resources	4	3	2	1
Databases	4	3	2	1
Computers and printers	4	3	2	1
Digital equipment	4	3	2	1
Computer software	4	3	2	1
Maker materials	4	3	2	1
Materials for school assignments	4	3	2	1
Materials for personal interests	4	3	2	1

Indicate Your Level of Agreement with the Following Statements:

I have adequate input into collection purchases.	Strongly agree	Agree	Disagree	Strongly disagree
There is adequate publicity about new purchases.	Strongly agree	Agree	Disagree	Strongly disagree
There are enough materials in the media center.	Strongly agree	Agree	Disagree	Strongly disagree
Materials in the collection are interesting.	Strongly agree	Agree	Disagree	Strongly disagree

The Library Should Purchase the Following:

What Improvements in the Collection or Access to Information Would You Find Most Useful?

STUDENT OPINIONS OF THE COLLECTION— BOOK TASTING AND SPEED DATING

School librarians are finding creative ways to enable students to voice their opinions about items in the collection while simultaneously introducing new books, genres of books, or subjects of books. One method is a book tasting (figure 3.3) where the library is set up like a restaurant with a variety

Appetizer	Main Course	Dessert
Name of book	Name of book	Name of book
Is the cover interesting? ☺ ☹	Is the cover interesting? ☺ ☹	Is the cover interesting? ☺ ☹
Read 3 pages of the book. What is it about?	Read 3 pages of the book. What is it about?	Read 3 pages of the book. What is it about?
What are some challenging words you found?	What are some challenging words you found?	What are some challenging words you found?
Would you check this book out? ☺ ☹	Would you check this book out? ☺ ☹	Would you check this book out? ☺ ☹
Who would like this book?	Who would like this book?	Who would like this book?

Figure 3.3 Book Tasting

Figure 3.3 Continued

of books at each table. Students preview (taste) each book for a few minutes and write short reviews on brochures that look like menus. In some cases, school librarians have heightened the experience for students by dressing up as chefs; decorating the tables with tablecloths, flowers, and placemats; and using seating reservations with name cards (Radcliff 2017).

Book speed dating (figure 3.4) functions in a similar manner but may be better suited to high schools. Students are given five minutes to preview each book before rotating to the next one, until they settle in with a book that is a good match (Lackey 2014). Pinterest is an excellent source for creative ideas on holding book tastings and book speed dating.

EVALUATION OF THE COLLECTION BY CHECKING CATALOGS, LISTS, AND BIBLIOGRAPHIES

A type of qualitative evaluation checks the library's collection against a variety of "best" lists. The following represents some of the most popular. (*Note:* Copyright dates are not provided in many instances because these are updated frequently.)

Catalogs

- Fiction Core Collection, H. W. Wilson (print) and EBSCO Information Services (online)
- Nonfiction Core Collection, H. W. Wilson (print) and EBSCO Information Services (online)
- Children's Core Collection, H. W. Wilson (print) and EBSCO Information Services (online)
- Middle & Junior High Core Collection, H. W. Wilson (print) and EBSCO Information Services (online)
- Senior High Core Collection, H. W. Wilson (print) and EBSCO Information Services (online)

Lists

- Best Fiction for Young Adults, Young Adult Library Services Association
- Quick Picks for Reluctant Readers, Young Adult Library Services Association
- Outstanding Books for the College Bound, Young Adult Library Services Association
- 100 Great Children's Books, 100 Years, New York Public Library
- Notable Children's Books, Booklist

Book Speed Dating

- First impressions time! Check out your date's cover and blurb. Open them up and look at the type, layout, and space.
- Get to know your date. Give your date full attention for three minutes.
- At the sound of the bell, fill in your sheet then move clockwise to the next table.

Table	Title	I'm in Love	It's OK	Not My Type
1				
2				
3				
4				
5				
6				

Were there any books you want to take on a second date? If so, borrow them at the counter.

Figure 3.4 Book Speed Dating

Table 3-6   Percentage of the Collection in Standard Sources

Fiction Collection	
Source title: _______________________________	
Number of fiction books in sample:	___________
Number of these titles found in source:	___________
Percent of titles found in source (b × 100)/a	___________
Nonfiction Collection	
Source title: _______________________________	
Number of nonfiction books in sample:	___________
Number of these titles found in source:	___________
Percent of titles found in source (b × 100)/a	___________
Percentage of entire collection found in standard sources	___________
(Average of each of the calculated percentages)	

Bibliographies

Bibliographies and book lists of recommended books on a wide range of themes and topics are available from the Children's Cooperative Book Center (CCBC) at the College of Education, University of Wisconsin–Madison.

A procedure that can be used to check the collection to see the percentage of titles that are available from standard bibliographies is feasible by using only a random sample of the collection. Use the master bar code list and check every twentieth bar code number on the list. A simple formula based on this methodology can be found in table 3.6.

You may wish to add further breakdowns to the form, such as biography, graphic novels, award winners, or easy books, or simply concentrate on one particular area of the collection.

EVALUATING THE COLLECTION AND INDIVIDUAL ITEMS FOR DIVERSITY

Social Justice Books, an organization that recommends antibias children's books, notes that "it is important to offer young children a range of books about people like them and their family—as well as about people who are different from them and their family. All of the books should be accurate and appealing to young children" (Derman-Sparks 2016). They offer the following "Guide for Selecting Anti-Bias Children's Books," which can also be used as a guide for evaluating existing books in the collection:

- Check the illustrations.
- Check the story line and relationships between people.
- Look at messages about different lifestyles.
- Consider the effects on children's self and social identities.
- Look for books about children and adults engaging in actions for change.
- Consider the author's or illustrator's background and perspective.
- Watch for loaded words.
- Look at the copyright date.
- Assess the appeal of the story and illustrations to young children.

In addition to evaluating individual books for bias, school librarians should also consider the balance of books in the library as a whole.

For accurate, authentic diversity with antibias values, a library or classroom must provide a combination of books that reflects the children, families, and communities of the program. Additional titles should depict diversity in the United States (and in the world as children get older). An antibias library maintains a balance of books that portray the following:

- A variety of ways of life. A range of families are depicted: urban, suburban, and rural; with or without financial resources; and with women and men in a wide range of roles.
- A wide range of family structures in stories that engage young children.
- Blue-collar workers, farmers, service workers, and artists as well as professionals and white-collar workers.
- Differently abled and able-bodied people actively taking initiative and filling a range of jobs and roles in the family.
- Diversity of looks, work, family, and way of life within all racial and ethnic groups.
- Able and differently abled children from all racial and ethnic groups, genders, and classes as active participants in the stories.
- Real people from all kinds of backgrounds—children and adults—engaged in actions for change, reflecting current lives as well as lives from the past. Past lives should include everyday people, not just famous individuals (Derman-Sparks 2016).

EVALUATION OF ELECTRONIC RESOURCES

It is recognized that there has been a shift from print to electronic resources in libraries. Students are accessing pay databases, e-books, and Internet sites to gather information. School librarians must not only evaluate these resources that must be purchased but also curate "free" open educational resources (OERs).

Journal Databases

The evaluation of usage of journal databases and e-books can be provided by vendors and may include the number of articles or chapters downloaded from journals or e-books and the number of times a database has been accessed. Examination of turnaway statistics may help libraries identify areas where the collection may not meet the needs of current users by identifying materials users wanted to access but were prohibited because the library did not have a library subscription (Johnson 2016). For example, the Gale Corporation (2019) provides the following usage reports:

> E-book Retrievals: Number of retrievals from individual e-book titles for a specific time frame
> Journal Retrievals: Number of retrievals from individual journal titles for a specific time frame
> Usage by Database: Usage by database for a specified time frame
> Usage by Location, Date, and Time: Pinpoints specific times users are accessing resources
> Usage by Session Time: Session count based on day and time
> Usage Summary: All Gale usage from a specific time frame rolled up into one number for searches, sessions, retrievals, and full-text retrievals

Open Education Resources

The use of open education resources (OERs) has been rapidly increasing over the past several years. The U.S. Department of Education is promoting the #GoOpen initiative, which encourages schools to transition to OERs to support their curricula. The Office of Educational Technology (2019) notes potential advantages to this transition:

> **Increase Equity:** All students have access to high quality learning materials that have the most up-to-date and relevant content because openly licensed educational resources can be freely distributed to anyone.
> **Keep Content Relevant and High Quality:** Traditional textbooks are perpetually outdated, forcing districts to re-invest significant portions of their budgets on replacing them. The terms of use of openly licensed educational resources allows educators to maintain the quality and relevance of their materials through continuous updates.
> **Empower Teachers:** Openly licensed educational resources empower teachers as creative professionals by giving them the ability to adapt and customize learning materials to meet the needs of their students without breaking copyright laws.
> **Save Money:** Switching to educational materials that are openly licensed enables schools to repurpose funding spent on textbooks for other

pressing needs, such as investing in the transition to digital learning. In some districts, replacing just one textbook has made tens of thousands of dollars available for other purposes.

School librarians, already proficient at selecting all types of resources, have taken a leadership role in curating OERs (Luetkemeyer 2017). Mifflin (2018) provides guidance on reliable means to evaluating OERs via the following resources:

- Various State Department of Education websites—preselected resources tied to the curriculum (e.g., Louisiana, https://www.louis libraries.org/alearningla)
- UnboundEd—standards-aligned resources (https://www.unbounded .org)
- Open-Up Resources—grades six to eight math curriculum (https:// im.openupresources.org)
- International Society for Technology in Education (ISTE)— publications, courses, and videos for educators to learn more about OER (https://www.iste.org/learn/open-educational-resources)
- MERLOT—a searchable database of curated open resources (https:// www.merlot.org/merlot/index.htm)

The Source Educational Evaluation Rubric developed by Turnitin (2018) is a functional tool for reviewing OERs for their potential value to the curriculum. The rubric is built on five criteria:

- *Authority*: Is the site well regarded, cited, and written by experts in the field?
- *Educational Value*: Does the site content help advance educational goals?
- *Intent*: Is the site a well-respected source of content intended to inform users?
- *Originality*: Is the site a source of original content and viewpoints?
- *Quality*: Is the site highly vetted with good coverage of the topical area?

EVALUATION OF MEDIA

A plethora of research studies have demonstrated the contribution of audiovisual media to student learning and enjoyment (Harper 2010). Videos, available on DVD and streaming, enable students to experience educational content from various perspectives and learning styles. The evaluation of children's media encompasses not only content but also the quality of the art, photography, and audio. Figure 3.5 is a comprehensive checklist for evaluating both of these.

THE DIG CHECKLIST FOR INCLUSIVE, HIGH-QUALITY CHILDREN'S MEDIA

Answer 'Yes' or 'No' to any question that is relevant to the media you are reviewing.

Content: Story, Information, and Activity

High-quality digital content for children supports learning and literacy, reflects diverse experiences, feeds curiosity, develops empathy, and provides accurate information in a creative way.

All Content

- ☐ Who is the narrator? What is the point of view?
- ☐ Can kids select or customize the point of view?
- ☐ Is the content, including the setting and characters, free of stereotypical representations?
- ☐ Does the content include atypical settings and/or underrepresented life experiences which both allow more kids to see themselves in the media?
- ☐ Can kids explore an unfamiliar location, region, or situation?
- ☐ Does the content introduce experiences in ways that entertain and teach about a topic in a creative way?
- ☐ Does the media include links to additional content or opportunities within the media itself for curious families to learn more about a topic, setting, culture, or experience which is new to them?
- ☐ Are characters diverse in their culture, ethnicity, language, gender, age, social classes, physical features, sexual orientation, and ability, reflecting today's diverse families?
- ☐ Are diverse characters meaningfully integrated as individuals?

Type of Content

Stories and Tales

- ☐ Is the story original or is the story a retelling of a traditional tale?
- ☐ If the story is a retelling of a traditional, indigenous tale, is a member(s) of the team an authority on the subject?

Figure 3.5   The Diverse and Inclusive Growth Checklist

Source: Created by Claudia Haines for the Kids Inclusive and Diverse Media Action Project (KIDMAP, https://joinkidmap.org).

90

☐ Do the creators have permission to retell the story, if applicable?

☐ Does the story diversify the media offerings for children? Or is it similar in its setting, plot, characters, activities, and information to what is already widely available?

☐ Does the media offer historical, cultural, or social context for the story that is different from the traditional offerings?

Non-fiction/Informational Media

☐ Is the content accurate?

☐ Is a member(s) of the team an authority on the subject?

☐ Are references included and easily accessible?

☐ Does the content provide a different perspective on a topic or share information in a new way?

☐ Is the content updated to reflect current research?

☐ Does the content support critical thinking skills?

☐ Is the content searchable?

Activity/Game

☐ Does the activity's setting(s) include multiple living situations, playspaces, or other meeting places? Or does the media acknowledge in some way that the one setting is one of many alternatives in a creative way?

☐ Is the activity unique to a particular audience? Are there appropriate instructions for those unfamiliar with the activity?

☐ Does the activity encourage creativity, making, and self-expression?

☐ Does the activity encourage multi-generational coviewing, coplay, and joint media engagement?

☐ Does the activity inspire connection with family and/or community members?

☐ Are there recommended resources, books for example, included with the media that extend the activity's learning experience?

Art

High-quality images, illustrations, video, and animations help create a richer experience for the user.

☐ Does the media include authentic visual representation of culturally and ethnically diverse characters, environments, and experiences?

☐ Do the artwork and images provide historical, social, or cultural context for the story, information, or activity?

Figure 3.5 Continued

☐ Do the artwork and images align with the text and narration?
☐ Do kids see themselves, their families, and/or their communities authentically depicted in the artwork and images?
☐ Are characters with different body types and abilities featured in various roles?
☐ Can kids customize characters' appearance?
  ○ Can they create their own avatar or choose from multiple characters?
  ○ Can they choose ethnicity, physical features, clothing, and accessories?
  ○ Can they choose gender or create a gender-neutral character?

Audio

High-quality digital media features music, narration, and sound that enrich the media experience.

☐ Does the media include multiple language options which are spoken/written by native speakers?
☐ Can children easily select and change languages while using the media?
☐ Does the narration align with the text and illustrations?
☐ Does the app feature a voice record option to support family participation in a variety of home languages?
☐ Does the media include music or sound effects culturally appropriate for the content?
☐ Does the music have any historical, social, cultural context?
☐ Can the music and sound effects be turned on/off to modify the experience for individual children?

Audience

High-quality digital media provides age-appropriate experiences for the intended audience. Some media addresses the specific needs of a particular, underserved audience while other media aims to include a wider audience in a common experience.

☐ Who is the intended audience?
☐ Are diverse families authentically represented in the media?
☐ Does the audience have opportunities to see themselves reflected in the content of the media?

Figure 3.5 Continued

☐ Does the audience have the opportunity to learn about and experience another culture, region, language, or ability in the content of the media?
☐ Does the media address the specific needs of a particular, underserved audience?
☐ Does the media include a wider audience in a common experience?
☐ Are the experiences age-appropriate for the intended audience?
☐ Are diverse families used in advertising/marketing images and messaging?
☐ Are the media's descriptions and ads available in multiple languages?

Purpose

☐ High-quality media aims to inform, entertain, teach, connect, and inspire all kids from all backgrounds.
☐ What is the media's purpose?
☐ Is authentic representation of diverse backgrounds, traditions, abilities, and rituals a part of the purpose?
☐ Is accessibility addressed in the media's purpose?
☐ Is the purpose, at least in part, to encourage multiple kids or multiple people to explore, learn, share, and create together?

Functionality & Navigation

High-quality digital media for kids includes technical features that support accessibility, successful learning, privacy, customization, and joint media engagement.

☐ Is the media glitch-free?
☐ Are in app-purchases, sharing features, and external links locked behind a "parental gate"?
☐ Is the media free of advertising?
☐ Is the media easy for kids and their grown ups with diverse abilities to use? Can they access all of the content?
☐ Was Universal Design for Learning a part of the overall design process?
☐ Does the media integrate age-appropriate cues for meaningful interactivity?
☐ Is the functionality connected to any representation of backgrounds, traditions, rituals and if so, is that representation authentic?
☐ Does the media allow the user to change settings or other elements, allowing the user to customize the experience?
☐ Do the technical features encourage coviewing and shared play?

Figure 3.5 Continued

☐ Can kids navigate to specific parts of the media, for example the home screen, favorite page or scene, specific part of a puzzle?

Instructions, Guides, and Support Materials for Grown-Ups

High-quality digital media for children includes tips, instructions, or a guide for grown-ups with suggested activities that make the media more accessible to more kids and potentially increase the educational value.

☐ Does the media offer grown-up tips, instructions, extension activities, or a guide?
☐ Are the tips, instructions, extension activities, or guide available in multiple languages?
☐ Do the supporting materials provide tips for encouraging bilingual development?
☐ Do the instructions and support materials feature a range of diverse characters?
☐ Does the guide offer suggestions on how to use the media to teach kids about diversity of all kinds?
☐ Do the instructions and support materials provide any historical, social, or cultural context for the content?
☐ Does the media protect kids' privacy?

Instructions, Guides, and Support Materials for Grown-Ups

High-quality digital media for children includes tips, instructions, or a guide for grown-ups with suggested activities that make the media more accessible to more kids and potentially increase the educational value.

☐ Does the media offer grown-up tips, instructions, extension activities, or a guide?
☐ Are the tips, instructions, extension activities, or guide available in multiple languages?
☐ Do the instructions and support materials feature a range of diverse characters?
☐ Do the instructions and support materials provide any historical, social, or cultural context for the content?
☐ Does the media protect kids' privacy?

Figure 3.5 Continued

Creative Team

A diverse team of creators, designers and developers with an array life experiences may design and develop a broader assortment of content that feature a variety of perspectives, characters, and settings.

- ☐ Who are the members of the creative team? Who is the author, illustrator, developer, educational or cultural consultant?
- ☐ Is information about the creators easily accessible?
- ☐ Is the artwork, story, music, and functionality created by a diverse team?
- ☐ Is a member of the team trained in Universal Design for Learning standards?

The DIG Checklist was created by Claudia Haines, Youth Services Librarian and creator of *Evaluating Apps and New Media for Young Children: A Rubric*. This tool has been fine-tuned with input from J. Elizabeth Mills (University of Washington), Tamara Kaldor (TEC Center at Erikson Institute), Kevin Clark, Ph.D. (Center for Digital Media Innovation and Diversity, George Mason University), Chip Donohue, Ph.D. (TEC Center at Erikson Institute), Warren Buckleitner (Children's Technology Review), Carissa Christner (Madison Public Library), Daryl Grabarek (School Library Journal), and Karen Nemeth (Language Castle). Stay tuned for more updates.

Figure 3.5   Continued

CIRCULATION ANALYSIS

Circulation statistics are the most conventional means of analyzing usage of the collection in school libraries. These statistics may be tabulated daily, weekly, or monthly and then cumulated at the end of the year. But for what purpose? Is circulation an accurate measure of use? Other than perpetual testing with a reading management program, can you determine whether a student has read or used the book he or she has taken out? Do circulation reports account for in-library use of materials and electronic resources? Are circulation statistics relevant when students are on fixed schedules, come to the library once a week, and check out two books each? Do circulation reports have meaning for principals? According to my research, circulation reports rank thirteenth out of fourteen in importance as a method that principals use to evaluate their school library programs (Everhart 2003).

Could it be that the manner in which circulation figures are presented holds little significance for principals? It could be more valuable to have circulation expressed in productivity measures that are straightforward to calculate:

$$\textbf{Circulation per Student} = \frac{\text{annual circulation}}{\text{number of students in the school}}$$

$$\textbf{Circulation per Hour} = \frac{\text{annual circulation}}{(\text{hours per day library is open}) \times (\text{days of school})}$$

True measures of circulation include number of loans, content downloaded, and in-house uses (ISO Standards 2018).

> A content download is defined as a content unit being successfully requested from a database, electronic serial or digital document. . . . Only downloads from the library's electronic collection are counted. This comprises all documents acquired or licensed by the library, but excludes free Internet resources, even if the library has included them in its online catalog. . . . Downloads indicate that users have found items that seem to be relevant to their interests. The measure could be seen in analogy to loans of print materials, while sessions could be seen in analogy to browsing the shelves. Therefore, downloads can be regarded as the most expressive measure for the relevance of the electronic collection to users. (Poll and Boekhorst 2008, 125, 171, 184)

School librarians can access the number of downloads via reports from their district's administrative or network infrastructure. Reports are also available from database providers.

In-House Use

The techniques already mentioned evaluate the usage of materials that have been checked out or downloaded. However, many times, students and teachers come into the library and use materials there without ever checking them out. There are several ways to evaluate in-house use of library materials:

- Examine materials left on tables, carrels, desks, or the floor.
- Scan the barcodes of materials left on tables, carrels, desks, or the floor to a patron designated as "in-house use."
- Interview users as they are leaving the library to find out which resources they used.
- Directly observe patrons using resources in-house.
- Design survey forms and leave them in volumes. When the volume is used, the patron fills out the form and deposits it in a central location.

During the time you are conducting your analysis of in-house use, you may want to post signs that read "Do not reshelve" or "Leave here" and place baskets or carts throughout the library. Again, it may only be necessary to collect data for a short period to make predictions for the entire year.

Annual Turnover Rate

Turnover rate is the average circulation per volume owned and is obtained through the following equation:

$$\textbf{Turnover Rate} = \frac{\text{annual circulation}}{\text{total library holdings}}$$

For example, if you have a collection of 30,000 items and your annual circulation is 150,000, your turnover rate would be 5, and it could be inferred that each item in the collection was checked out 5 times. "Although there are no established or agreed-upon standards for collection turnover rates, most public libraries like to see the material in their collections turn over (or get used) anywhere from 6 to 10 times a year" (Disher 2014, 33).

The following are further interpretations of turnover rate (Van House et al. 1987):

High Turnover Rate

- The library has a high circulation of materials compared to the collection size.
- A collection of mainly high-interest, circulating materials will have a high turnover rate.

Low Turnover Rate

- A library with a wide range of materials, including less popular titles, or with a large noncirculating reference collection will have a lower turnover rate.
- High in-library use and a low turnover rate may mean that materials tend to be used inside rather than outside the library.
- A library with a large proportion of out-of-date or inappropriate materials will have a low turnover rate.

Relative Use Factor

One might expect that circulation in each area of the collection will be somewhat in line with the representation of that section as a whole. "For example, if fiction represents 20 percent of the collection, does it also represent 20 percent of circulation? While that does not hold exactly true (the easy readers will usually circulate much more than their proportionate size relative to the whole collection), knowing the percentages can help you determine where extra work may be needed" (North Texas Regional Library System 2018). Reports can be run to calculate the relative use factor:

$$\textbf{Relative Use Factor} = \frac{\text{percentage of circulation}}{\text{percentage of collection responsible for that circulation}}$$

However, calculating the percentage of circulation for various segments of the collection does not tell the whole story. Because each of these areas contains differing numbers of volumes, the percentages may be deceiving. For example, if there are five hundred circulations in the 500s as well as five hundred circulations in the 900s, the percentage of circulations would be identical. But if there were two thousand volumes in the 500s and three thousand in the 900s, the actual use in both areas is unequal.

The relative use factor takes into account both the percentage of circulations in a given area as well as the percentage of items in that area to provide a more balanced view (Lancaster 1988). A relative use factor of 1 would mean that area of the collection is being used in direct proportion to the number of items available. Consequently, a relative use factor of less than

1 means the collection is being underutilized in that area, and a relative use factor greater than 1 means the items are being more heavily used.

A word of caution: when a broad classification has a very high relative use factor, this does not necessarily mean that the entire class is being heavily used. It is a good idea to break down the classification even further (which is possible on most automated circulation systems) to see where the exact use is. For example, the 700s may have a relative use factor of 2.15, but the books in music and sports have factors of 0.8 and 2.9, respectively.

Nonuse

Nonuse refers to the percentage of materials in the collection that have not been used in-house or circulated. It is determined with the following equation:

$$\text{Nonuse} = \frac{\text{Total number of items never circulated (circulation} = 0)}{\text{Total number of items in the collection}}$$

Items that have a circulation of zero can be determined by running a report and then counting the number of items. If a library has a high percentage of nonuse, the collection is not being used effectively. Similar recommendations and conclusions as noted for the relative use factor above can be applied.

Fill Rate

One of the major problems with the circulation statistics previously mentioned is that there is no way of knowing whether the materials taken out actually reflect what the user wanted. To calculate this, users must be surveyed. The resulting statistic, called the *fill rate*, is defined as the percentage of successful searches for library materials in any part of the library collection, and it is calculated by dividing the number of successful searches by all searches (Walter 1992). Directions for determining the fill rate for children in public libraries are adapted and simplified here from Walter (1992) for schools (see the Fill Rate Survey on pages 100–101):

- Take the sample survey during two different times of the year.
- You must be able to collect and count at least one hundred surveys. Duplicate enough forms.
- Target every child that comes into the library.
- Number the forms so you will know how many were given out.
- Post signs announcing that a survey is being conducted.

Form # _________________________________

How old are you? __________

Were you looking for anything special in the library?   YES   NO

   Please tell what us you were looking for:

a.   ____

     Did you find it?   YES   NO

b.   ____

     Did you find it?   YES   NO

c.   ____

     Did you find it?   YES   NO

3.   If you were just browsing and not looking for anything special, did you find anything
     interesting?   YES   NO

4.   Is there anything else you want to tell us about the library? You may write on the back of the
     page if you want to.

Thank you for answering our questions.
Please leave this form with the librarian today.

TITLE, SUBJECT, AUTHOR (1)   BROWSING (2)

Form Number   Found (a)   Not found (b)   Browsers (a)   Found Something (b)

TOTALS

FILL RATE:

1.   Title/subject/authors sought (total of columns 1a and 1b)   __________

2.   Title/subject/authors found (total of column 1a)   __________

3.   Title/subject/authors fill rate (line 2 divided by line 1)   __________

4.   Number of browsers (total of column 2a)   __________

5.   Number of browsers finding something (total of column 2b)   __________

6.   Browsing fill rate (line 5 divided by line 4)   __________

7.   Total fill rate (total of lines 2 and 5 divided by total of lines 1 and 4)   __________

Note: (form should be extended to include additional form numbers and results)

- Place clearly marked collection boxes for completed forms in strategic locations—the circulation desk, the reference desk (if separate), and by the exits.
- It is not enough to simply have the forms available to take. Either a staff member or a volunteer should make contact with each student. Much of the success of this process depends on how this person approaches the patrons. It can be very empowering for children to be asked for their input. The survey distributor may say something like, "The library wants to know if you are finding what you need here. Please fill this out and help us serve you better." Be assertive and friendly but not overbearing.
- Although the form is very simple, children under the age of eight will likely need help filling it out. It is all right for a staff member or volunteer to interview the child and write down the information.

The fill rate tells you the probability that a search will be successful (Walter 1992). For example, a 78 percent fill rate means that a student has a 78 percent chance of finding something he or she is looking for. If the fill rate is low and the circulation is high, it may mean that the collection is heavily used. Low fill rates may mean the library is underused or has a large noncirculating collection (which is becoming more and more common with the use of digital resources). Focus group interviews may clarify the percentage calculated.

Walter (1992) suggests these strategies to increase fill rates:

- Reexamine your collection development policy; perhaps you need to add more duplicate copies of popular titles or work harder to determine and meet user needs.
- Make your collection easier to use by arranging it differently or adding better signage.
- Offer more effective assistance in using the collection. Perhaps the staff needs some additional training in providing readers' advisory service to young library users, or perhaps the staff needs to be more visible.

Cost-Effectiveness Measures

Once you have calculated your annual circulation, you can use this number to construct some other output measures based on finances (Everhart 2003). These measures may be of particular interest to administrators and parents.

$$\textbf{Cost per Use} = \frac{\text{library budget}}{\text{annual circulation}}$$

$$\text{Cost per Search in a Database} = \frac{\text{cost of the database}}{\text{number of searches in that database}}$$

$$\text{Database Cost per Student} = \frac{\text{cost of database}}{\text{the student population}}$$

Low cost per use would generally be considered as showing high cost-effectiveness of the library. "It is for the library to decide what it regards as a good cost-benefit relation—there are no generally applicable standards. If the cost per session seems too high, the library could either promote the use of the electronic resource, for example, in user training, or cancel it" (Poll and Boekhorst 2008, 185).

EVALUATION OF THE COLLECTION BY CHECKING STUDENTS' SOURCES

School librarians can gain valuable information on which resources students actually use for assignments by systematically checking their bibliographies. Known as *citation analysis* or *bibliometrics*, this user-centered method could be used to determine the number and types of resources used and their age, for example. A coding sheet, similar to that in table 3.7, can streamline the process.

Some questions that could be asked after the coding include the following:

- What types of resources did students use when they were given prior instruction? What types did they use when they were not given prior instruction?
- What percentage of resources that were used are available in the school library?

Table 3-7 Coding Sheet for Students' Bibliographies

Case No.	Total Book References	Total Paid Database References	Total Free Internet Resources	Total References

Teacher	Average Date of Books	Average Date of Database References	Average Date of Internet References	Average Date of All References

- What resources were not from the library?
- Which resources are cited most often?

Results can be used to plan future lessons or order needed materials.

REFERENCES

American Association of School Librarians (AASL). 2018. *National School Library Standards for Learners, School Librarians, and School Libraries.* Chicago: ALA Editions.

American Library Association (ALA). 2018. "Selection Criteria." Last modified January. http://www.ala.org/tools/challengesupport/selectionpolicy toolkit/criteria.

Derman-Sparks, Louise. 2016. "Guide for Selecting Anti-Bias Children's Books." Social Justice Books. https://socialjusticebooks.org/guide-for -selecting-anti-bias-childrens-books.

Disher, Wayne. 2014. *Crash Course in Collection Development.* 2nd ed. Santa Barbara, CA: Libraries Unlimited.

Everhart, Nancy. 2003. "Evaluation of School Library Media Centers: Demonstrating Quality." *Library Media Connection* 21 (6): 14–21. ERIC (EJ671766).

Follett School Solutions. 2019. "Titlewave." www.titlewave.com.

Gale Corporation. 2019. "Gale Usage Reporting Overview." Last modified March 14. https://support.gale.com/doc/usage.

Harper, Meghan. 2010. "Linking Audiovisuals with Multicultural Literature." In *Multicultural Literature and Response: Affirming Diverse Voices*, edited by Lynn Atkinson Smolen and Ruth A. Oswald, 357–70. Columbus, OH: Linworth Publishing.

Intner, Sheila S., and Elizabeth Futas. 1994. "Evaluating Public Library Collections: Why Do It, and How to Use the Results." *American Libraries* 25 (5): 410–12. http://www.jstor.org/stable/25633247.

ISO Standards. 2018. "ISO 2789:2013(En), Information and Documentation— International Library Statistics." https://www.iso.org/obp/ui/#iso:std:iso :2789:ed-5:v1:en.

Johnson, Qiana. 2016. "Moving from Analysis to Assessment: Strategic Assessment of Library Collections." *Journal of Library Administration* 56 (4): 488–98. doi:10.1080/01930826.2016.1157425.

Lackey, Susie. 2014. "Get On Board the Book Speed Dating Train: Programming for Teens." *School Library Journal*, March 4. https://www.slj.com?detailStory=get-on-board-the-book-speed-dating-train-programming-for-teens.

Lancaster, F. W. 1988. *If You Want to Evaluate Your Library*. Champaign: University of Illinois Press.

Luetkemeyer, Jennifer R. 2017. "Are School Librarians Ready to Lead Mandated Digital Integration? A Survey of Florida's K–12 School Library Professionals." *School Libraries Worldwide* 23 (1): 56–83. doi:10.14265.23.1.005.

Mackin Educational Resources. 2018. "Collection Management." https://www.mackin.com/hq/library-services/collection-management.

Mardis, Marcia. 2016. *The Collection Program in Schools: Concepts and Practices*. 6th ed. Santa Barbara, CA: ABC-CLIO.

Maryland State Department of Education. 1987. *Building Library Media Collections: Analysis of Client Groups*. Baltimore: Maryland State Department of Education.

Mifflin, Lawrie. 2018. "How to Sort the Good from the Bad in OER." *Hechinger Report*, March 14. https://hechingerreport.org/how-to-sort-the-good-from-the-bad-in-oer.

North Texas Regional Library System. 2018. *Evaluating Your Collection: Best Practices for North Texas Libraries*. https://fliphtml5.com/vkdv/dsbz.

Office of Educational Technology. 2019. "Open Education." https://tech.ed.gov/open.

Poll, Roswitha, and Peter te Boekhorst. 2008. *Measuring Quality: Performance Measurement in Libraries*. 2nd rev. ed. Munich: De Gruyter Saur.

Radcliff, Dianna. 2017. "Host a Book Tasting!" *Sassy, Savvy, Simple Teaching* (blog), Last modified January 1. https://www.sassysavvysimpleteaching.com/2017/01/host-a-book-tasting.

School Library Journal. 2019. "SLJ's Average Book Prices for 2019."
March 11. https://www.slj.com/?detailStory=slj-average-book-prices-2019.

Texas State Library and Archives Commission. 2012. *CREW: A Weeding
Manual for Modern Libraries.* Revised by Jeanette Larson. Austin: Texas
State Library and Archives Commission. https://www.tsl.texas.gov/sites
/default/files/public/tslac/ld/ld/pubs/crew/crewmethod12.pdf.

Texas State Library and Archives Commission and the Texas Education
Agency. 2017. *School Library Programs: Standards and Guidelines for
Texas.* Revised August 2017. Austin: Texas State Library and Archives
Commission. https://www.tsl.texas.gov/sites/default/files/public/tslac/ld
/schoollibs/sls/Texas%20School%20Library%20Standards%20E
-Version%20FINAL.pdf.

Turnitin. 2018. "Source Evaluation Rubric." https://go.turnitin.com/seer
-rubric.

Van House, Nancy, Mary Jo Lynch, Charles R. McClure, Douglas L.
Zweizig, and Eleanor Rodger. 1987. *Output Measures for Public Librar-
ies: A Manual of Standardized Procedures.* 2nd ed. Chicago: American
Library Association.

Walter, Virginia A. 1992. *Output Measures for Public Library Service to
Children: A Manual of Standardized Procedures.* Chicago: American
Library Association.

Chapter 4

Facilities

The school library facility forms the first impression of the library program, and its importance cannot be overemphasized. Impression management theory states that individuals and organizations must establish and maintain impressions that are congruent with the perceptions they want to convey to the public (Hass 1981). What impression do you want to convey about your school library? Does one feel invited or unwelcome? Does visiting the library make students and teachers want to come back? According to Joan Frye Williams (2006), when people enter a school library, they ask themselves: "(1) Is this my kind of place? (2) Can I be successful here? and (3) Does this place fit with the rest of my life?" (ii, quoted in Mardis 2011). Recent research and anecdotal information (Loh 2016; Altobelli 2017; Kosciw et al. 2018) has drawn attention to how school libraries are more than physical places; rather, they are social and affective spaces where children and young adults seek safety from bullying and discrimination. Beyond the psychological aspects, the satisfaction with the design and aesthetics of schools and classrooms (and, by extension, school libraries) have a relationship with student academic engagement (Scott-Webber, Konyndyk, and French 2019).

Oftentimes, evaluation of the facility is overlooked because school librarians feel there is nothing they can do—the facility cannot be moved or enlarged. Although this is certainly true, there are many other aspects in regard to the facility that can be evaluated and should be. An evaluation may be the first step in convincing administrators that changes are necessary to achieve educational goals.

SCHOOL LIBRARY CLIMATE

Students and teachers are not the only ones who make judgments based on the library environment. Principals evaluate their school librarians most frequently (even above their teaching ability) by informally visiting the school library and observing the facilities (Everhart 2006). They form positive opinions based on the following:

- There is an organized, clean, inviting environment.
- Students are "actively engaged" with books or technology.
- The librarian is interacting with teachers and students.
- A variety of materials are available.
- There are relevant displays.
- Students are borrowing books.

Although climate is a topic addressed sparingly in the literature for school librarians, the New York State Education Department's (2016) School Library Evaluation Rubric provides a category for ascertaining climate.

Climate Conducive to Learning
Distinguished

- A stimulating environment makes the library media program a focal point of learning; library media program resources invite discovery, motivating projects, independent study; a variety of spaces accommodate different learning styles; library media program provides access to individuals with disabilities and resources in different levels and languages; administration is engaged.

Proficient

- Library media program provides respectful environment; users feel welcome to research, read, work independently; library media program is active in meeting user needs; space is organized, easy to navigate, resources are at different levels, sometimes accessible to individuals with disabilities. Administrative behavior is supportive.

Basic

- Library media program is quiet, clean, functional, used mainly for classes; students work to fulfill assignments, but rarely visit on their own. Library media program is reactive in meeting user needs; there is limited variety of resources at various levels, with accessibility in development. Administrative behavior is moderately supportive to indifferent.

Below Basic

- Library media program climate is closed and uninviting, students do not feel welcome, and teacher and administrator behavior is disengaged. Library media program is either rule bound or has no rules; library media program is inactive in meeting student needs; resource variety is highly limited, with little concern for accessibility.

Gower, Beal, and Loewecke (2018) provide other best practices related to school library climate:

- Create a centrally located, friendly service point.
- Include a self-check station for kids to check out their own materials.
- Engage in good merchandising techniques near the main service point by incorporating child-friendly signage and/or incorporating face-out merchandising throughout the area.
- Include digital signage to highlight programs and events for caregivers and older children that will bring them back for new library experiences.

EXISTING FACILITIES

Few school librarians are fortunate enough to be in on the inception of a building program whereby you can plan a new library facility. Most must operate within constraints they have been given and make the best of the situation. After working in the same facility year after year, you may not see it clearly. In evaluating school library media center facilities, one must take a step back and approach the center like a user. Fortunately, there is an array of techniques, surveys, and forms to assist in this task. These can be used by school librarians, administrators, or peers whom you enlist to evaluate your facility with fresh eyes.

In the past, there have been clear quantitative guidelines as to how large the school library should be, what specific areas it should contain, and the furniture and equipment that should be in those areas. Modern thinking, as reflected in state, local, and international standards, is that the school library facility should provide spaces for students to think, create, share, and grow (AASL 2018). The International Federation of Library Associations and Institutions (2015) maintains that the following functional areas need to be provided:

- *Study and research area*—space for information desk, catalogues, online stations, study and research tables, reference materials, and basic collections.

- *Informal reading area*—space for books and periodicals that encourage literacy, lifelong learning, and reading for pleasure.
- *Instructional area*—space with seats catering for small groups, large groups, and whole classroom formal instruction, with appropriate instructional technology and display space. (Seating for 10 percent of the student population is often recommended).
- *Media production and group project area*—space for individuals, teams, and classes (often called *labs* or *makerspaces*).
- *Administrative area*—space for circulation desk and office area, space for processing of library media materials, and storage space for equipment, supplies, and materials. (33)

LEARNING COMMONS

"While every library learning commons is a school library, not every school library is ready to be called a library learning commons" (Ekdahl, Zubke, and Daly 2017, 3). Learning commons are dynamic, collaborative spaces that incorporate mobile tables, shelving, and stackable chairs, allowing for transformation of space for multiple uses. Franz (2016) describes the functional areas as zones:

1. *The Collaborative Zone*
   This zone is focused on project-based learning and group work. Teamwork, multimedia collaboration, and displays of student work are encouraged. Tables can easily be moved and reconfigured. Seating options should be lightweight so that they can be easily picked up and rearranged to encourage spontaneous collaboration. Power access and connectivity are important considerations. Charging stations and in-table outlets are handy for students who want to charge their devices, and media tables allow students and instructors to plug in and share their screens.

2. *The Social Learning Zone*
   What distinguishes this zone from collaboration is that it is meant to be more playful, casual, and comfortable. It may take on a living room feel with ample soft seating and a variety of work surfaces. For example, café tables and stools contribute to a relaxed coffee shop appeal. Students are encouraged to interact with each other here. Embrace noise and conversation in this area.

3. *The Individual Study Zone*
   This zone is for students who want to study or work on their own. Often, students do not mind doing their own thing in the presence of others who may be talking or working together. In this regard, there do not have to be wide margins of separation between this zone and the other ones. However, there should still be some privacy elements.

In evaluating learning commons, one approach is simple reflection based on learning commons characteristics such as collaborative and participatory environments, responsive dynamics and professional leadership, as prescribed by Loertscher and Koechlin (2014). Analyze each of the characteristics by asking yourself: Where am I now? Where do I want to go? How will I get there?

EVALUATING SPECIFIC ASPECTS OF FACILITIES

Makerspaces

The popularity of makerspaces has necessitated that they be evaluated to find out what is working and what is not. Some methods and measures reported in the literature (Jensen 2016; Gerstein and Bray 2017; *School Library Journal* 2017) include the following:

Observation

_____ Total users per day

_____ Return visits

_____ Student engagement (for the entire period; a-ha moments, products they are proud of, attempting different projects, using critical thinking)

_____ Popularity by type (coding, digital design, building, arts and crafts, etc.)

_____ Photographs

User Feedback

_____ Suggestion box

_____ Interviews

_____ Visitor logs

_____ Exit surveys/self-reflective forms

_____ Journals

Program Evaluation

_____ Products

_____ Process

_____ Activities that are related to curriculum

_____ Collaboration with teachers

Output Measures

_____ **Level of student involvement** $= \dfrac{\text{total number of users}}{\text{student population}}$

_____ **Cost per user** $= \dfrac{\text{total number of users}}{\text{annual makerspace funding}}$

Signage

Signs can set the tone for a friendly or hostile environment and a helpful or confusing library visit. To be effective, signage must be consistent, concise, and free of jargon and punitive language. Students have noted they are aided in libraries by signs that are uniform in size and font (Hahn and Zitron 2011). According to the U.S. Americans with Disabilities Act (ADA) guidelines, signs at a distance of one hundred feet should have characters four inches high. Overhead signage should have three-inch-high characters when suspended eighty feet. The following color combinations are recommended for clear signs (Schoeneck 2014):

Backgrounds	**Text**
Black	White, Yellow
Red	White, Yellow
White	Black, Red, Blue, and Gray
Yellow	Black, Red, Blue, and Gray
Green	White, Yellow, and Beige
Blue	White, Yellow

School libraries can contain many signs of all types—directional, informational, and instructional. A recent study found that a typical elementary school library has 203 signs, a middle school library has 93, and a high school library has 139 (Mandel and Johnston 2019).

An efficient evaluation of signage should include a complete inventory of existing signage, including an analysis of the types of signs and their location, language, and design (Stempler and Polger 2013). Such an evaluation system for school libraries has been developed by Mandel and Johnston (2019). The school library signage worksheets shown in figures 4.1–4.3 can guide you.

EVALUATING HOW STUDENTS USE LIBRARY SPACE

School librarians can better understand student behavior and subsequently improve user experience within the physical library space by choosing to capture what we call space use data (Gullikson and Meyer 2016).

Tracking and measuring items that are interacted with is much easier than trying to tell what people are doing inside a space. When someone checks out a book, clicks a link on a database, or walks through the door, that's a fairly easy action to measure. Answering more complicated questions about library use is much harder.

SIGN NAME	CATEGORY					LOCATION					LANG LEVEL APPROP		ISSUES						NOTES
	Directional		Regulatory		Info											damage			
	→	Text	Lib	Other		table	stack end	shelf	wall	other	yes	no	not clear	wrong loctn	not current	sign	holder	other (specify)	

Figure 4.1 School library signage worksheet

Source: Mandel, Lauren H., and Melissa P. Johnston. 2019. "Evaluating Library Signage: A Systematic Method for Conducting a Library Signage Inventory." Journal of Librarianship & Information Science 51 (1): 150. doi: 10.1177/0961000616681837.

Main Category	Subcategory	Definition
Sign Name		Name of the sign derived from text on the sign
Category	Directional →	Signs that indicate direction by use of arrows
	Directional Tx	Signs that indicate direction by use of text
	Reg – L	Signs that indicate library rules
	Reg – O	Signs that indicate non-library rules
	Inf	All other signs
Location	Table	Sign on a table or desk
	Stack end	Sign on the end of a bookstack
	Shelf	Sign on a shelf
	Wall	Sign on a wall
	Other (specify)	Sign in another location, such as on a computer monitor
Age Approp	Yes	Sign is in language level appropriate to school level
	No	Sign is not in language level appropriate to school level
Issues	Not clear	Sign that is not clear but not because it is too small, has too much text, or has text that is too small
	Wrng loctn	Sign that is not where it belongs
	Placement	Sign is placed poorly, for example crookedly
	Not current	Sign that is outdated
	Damage – sign	Sign that is damaged
	Damage – holder	Sign holder that is damaged
	Poor color	Sign uses color that is hard to read such as yellow text on white background
	Other (specify)	Any other issue
Notes		Any comments or elaboration necessary

Figure 4.2 School library signage worksheet

Source: Mandel, Lauren H., and Melissa P. Johnston. 2019. "Evaluating Library Signage: A Systematic Method for Conducting a Library Signage Inventory." Journal of Librarianship & Information Science 51 (1): 150. doi: 10.1177/0961000616681837.

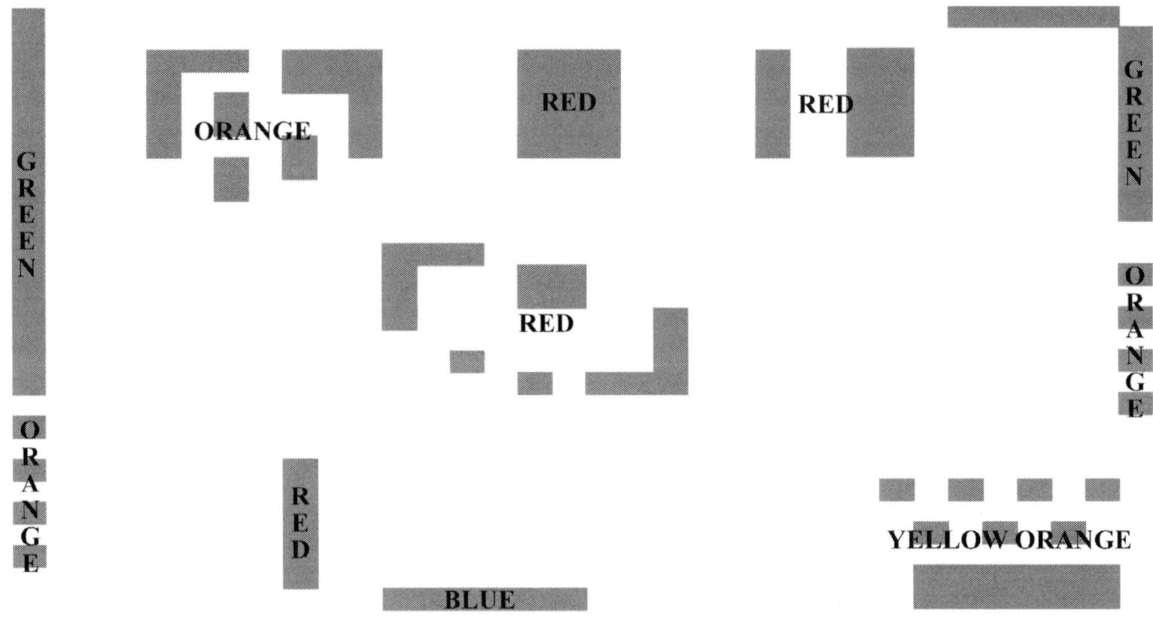

Figure 4.3 Library heat map

Source: Mandel, Lauren H., and Melissa P. Johnston. 2019. "Evaluating Library Signage: A Systematic Method for Conducting a Library Signage Inventory." Journal of Librarianship & Information Science 51 (1): 150. doi: 10.1177/0961000616681837.

What do patrons pay attention to as they walk through the building? Where do patrons choose to sit, and, more importantly, why do they choose those specific places? Are your spaces more conducive to people sitting by themselves or in groups? How do groups affect other uses of the library? (Griffey 2018, 6)

Evaluating how students use library space is best carried out unobtrusively.

The basic premise behind the use of unobtrusive measures is that you can learn a great deal about the library and its use by looking at how things wear ("erosion"), how things are left in the building ("traces"), and how things are rearranged ("adaptations for use") (Harris and Schweighardt 2017). Erosion tells you that activity has taken place in a certain spot or area. Examples of erosion in a school library may include the following:

- Worn spots in the carpet or tile
- Paint, varnish, or upholstery worn off furniture
- Wear on library books, especially on corners where the page is turned or on spines
- Markings in books
- Letters/numbers worn off computer keys

Traces are physical evidence of use left around the library. Consider these traces:

- Fingerprints
- Food
- Litter
- Graffiti or carvings
- Dirt from shoes
- Dust on books (evidence of nonuse)
- Things left running on computer screens
- Books left on tables
- Stools or steps left by shelves

Finally, adaptations of use can tell you about the success or failure of some aspect of the facility. Library users make adaptations to modify the environment more to their liking, possibly indicating the environment did not serve its original intentions very well or that users impose different intentions. Most examples of adaptations of use in school libraries involve moving furniture around or using furniture for something other than its intended purpose.

Students' library space use is mainly determined by their spatial choices. These space attributes have been shown to have the greatest influence on students' spatial choices—amount of space, noise level, crowdedness, comfort of furnishing, and cleanliness (Gullikson and Meyer 2016). Understanding students' use of a library can be determined by a simple walk-through or as detailed as heat mapping or behavior mapping, which are systematic techniques for recording detailed observations.

Heat maps, as shown in figure 4.3, represent data in terms of color on a map or diagram. Lower values are typically represented by blue and higher values by red. Taken from a study of an academic library (Khoo et al. 2014), a heat map is constructed by doing the following:

1. Create a map or floor plan of the school library. The map should be detailed and include furnishings and all physical elements.
2. Divide each area into a series of zones that are coherent in terms of activity or furniture.
3. Give each zone a numerical identifier.
4. Make observations as to occupancy. Conduct multiple observations (at least one hundred) over numerous time periods.
5. Calculate the average occupancy percentage of each zone:

$$\textbf{average occupancy rate} = \frac{100 \times \text{average recorded occupancy}}{\text{maximum potential occupancy}}$$

6. Rank order the zones.
7. Color code the rank order.
8. Place colored zones on map.

Going beyond simple use, school librarians may wish to examine behavior in their spaces. Instructions for building a behavior map, as shown in figure 4.5, include the following:

1. Create a map or floor plan of the school library as above. Most maps used in this method have a grid marking each square foot.
2. Decisde on categories of behavior to be recorded. This is a critical state because it defines the types and magnitudes of behavior that will be noted by the evaluators. Behaviors might include things like talking, reading, walking, sleeping, and so forth.
3. Give each behavior a code or discrete abbreviation.
4. Observe the area under study, and using codes, record each behavior and time frame on the map. (Lushington and Kusack 1991)

Understanding students' use of space can facilitate effective design and planning, which in turn will result in more efficient use of space.

REFERENCES

Altobelli, Rachel, 2017. "Creating Space for Agency." *Knowledge Quest* 46 (1): 8–15. ERIC (EJ1153330).

American Association of School Librarians (AASL). 2018. *National School Library Standards for Learners, School Librarians, and School Libraries*. Chicago: ALA Editions.

Ekdahl, Moira, Sylvia Zubke, and Heather Daly, eds. 2017. *From School Library to Library Learning Commons: A Pro-Active Model for Educational Change*. Vancouver: British Columbia Teacher-Librarians' Association. https://bctladotca.files.wordpress.com/2018/02/from-school-library-to-library-learning-commons.pdf.

Everhart, Nancy. 2006. "Principals' Evaluation of School Librarians: A Study of Strategic and Nonstrategic Evidence-Based Approaches." *School Libraries Worldwide* 12 (2): 38–51. https://iasl-online.org/Resources/Documents/slw/v12/12_2everhart.pdf.

Franz, Rosalie. 2016. "Library as Learning Commons: 3 Key Zones." *Demco Ideas and Inspiration* (blog), October 17. https://ideas.demco.com/blog/library-learning-commons.

Gerstein, Jackie, and Barbara Bray. 2017. "Design Thinking Process and UDL Planning Tool for STEM, STEAM, Maker Education," *User Generated Education* (blog), June 8. https://usergeneratededucation.wordpress.com/2017/06/08/design-thinking-process-and-udl-planning-tool-for-stem-steam-maker-education.

Gower, Stephen, Amber Beal, and Angela Loewecke. 2018. "Checklist: Designing Engaging Library Spaces for Children," *Demco Interiors* (blog), October 19. https://www.demcointeriors.com/blog/designing-library-spaces-for-children.

Griffey, Jason. 2018. "Introduction." In *Library Spaces and Smart Buildings: Technology, Metrics, and Iterative Design*, 5–10. Chicago: ALA TechSource. doi:10.5860/ltr.54n1.

Gullikson, Shelley, and Kristin Meyer. 2016. "Collecting Space Use Data to Improve the UX of Library Space." *Weave: Journal of Library User Experience* 1 (5). doi:10.3998/weave.12535642.0001.502.

Hahn, Jim, and Lizz Zitron. 2011. "How First-Year Students Navigate the Stacks: Implications for Improving Wayfinding." *Reference & User*

Services Quarterly 51 (1): 28–35. https://journals.ala.org/index.php/rusq /article/viewFile/3558/3849.

Harris, Paul B., and Stephanie N. Schweighardt. 2017. "A Place to Think, Feel, and Act: Psychological Approaches to Understanding Library Spaces." In *Assessing Library Space for Learning*, edited by Susan E. Montgomery, 29–47. Lanham, MD: Rowman & Littlefield. eBook Collection, EBSCOhost (1531814).

Hass, Glen R. 1981. "Presentational Strategies, and the Social Expression of Attitudes: Impression Management within Limits." In *Impression Management Theory and Social Psychological Research*, edited by James T. Tedeschi, 127–46. New York: Academic Press.

IFLA School Libraries Section Standing Committee. 2015. *IFLA School Library Guidelines*. 2nd ed. Edited by Barbara Schultz-Jones and Dianne Oberg. The Hague: International Federation of Library Associations and Institutions. https://www.ifla.org/publications/node/9512.

Jensen, Karen. 2016. "MakerSpace: How Do You Evaluate This New Service?" *Teen Librarian Toolbox* (blog), *School Library Journal*, April 29. http://www.teenlibrariantoolbox.com/2016/04/makerspace-how-do-you -evaluate-this-new-service.

Khoo, Michael John, Lily Rozaklis, Catherine Hall, Diana Kusunoki, and Michael Rehrig. 2014. "Heat Map Visualizations of Seating Patterns in an Academic Library." *iConference 2014 Proceedings*: 612–20. doi:10.9776/14274.

Kosciw, Joseph G., Emily A. Greytak, Adrian D. Zongrone, Caitlin M. Clark, and Nhan L. Truong. 2018. *The 2017 National School Climate Survey: The Experiences of Lesbian, Gay, Bisexual, Transgender, and Queer Youth in Our Nation's Schools*. New York: GLSEN. https://www .glsen.org/sites/default/files/GLSEN-2017-National-School-Climate -Survey-NSCS-Full-Report.pdf.

Loertscher, David L., and Carol Koechlin. 2014. "Climbing to Excellence: Defining Characteristics of Successful Learning Commons." *Knowledge Quest* 42 (4): E1–E10.

Loh, Chin Le. 2016. "Levelling the Reading Gap: A Socio-Spatial Study of School Libraries and Reading in Singapore." *Literacy* 50 (1): 3–13. doi:10.1111/lit.12067.

Lushington, Nolan, and James Michael Kusack. 1991. *The Design and Evaluation of Public Library Buildings.* Hamden, CT: Library Professional Publications.

Mandel, Lauren H., and Melissa P. Johnston. 2019. "Evaluating Library Signage: A Systematic Method for Conducting a Library Signage Inventory." *Journal of Librarianship & Information Science* 51 (1): 150. doi:10.1177/0961000616681837.

Mardis, Marcia. 2011. "Reflections on School Library as Space, School Library as Place." *School Libraries Worldwide* 17 (1): I–III. ProQuest (847667248).

New York State Education Department. 2016. *School Library Media Program Evaluation.* New York: New York State Education Department. http://www.nysed.gov/common/nysed/files/programs/school-library -services/slmpe-rubric-2016.pdf.

Schoeneck, Angie. 2014. "Signage as a Component of Your Space Design, Merchandising and Service Models," *Demco Ideas and Inspiration* (blog), October 3. https://ideas.demco.com/blog/library-signs.

School Library Journal. 2017. "SLJ Research Reports for Download." Last modified July 17. https://www.slj.com/?detailStory=research.

Scott-Webber, Lennie, Rodger Konyndyk, and Raechel French. 2019. "Developing Instruments: Student Academic Engagement Levels and Satisfaction with School Design." *European Scientific Journal* 15 (1): 325. doi:10.19044/esj.2019.v15n1p325.

Stempler, Amy F., and Mark Aaron Polger. 2013. "Do You See the Signs? Evaluating Language, Branding, and Design in a Library Signage Audit." *Public Services Quarterly* 9 (2): 121–35. doi:10.1080/15228959.2013 .785881.

Chapter 5

Students

STUDENT EVALUATION OF THE LIBRARY

The most important part of any school library program is the students. However, unlike public libraries that seek input from their users, school libraries do not often ask students for their opinions. An anonymous survey of students is useful for getting honest feedback. There are many types of questions you can ask. The questions will obviously be related to what you are trying to evaluate. This general survey can be adapted for different grade levels, broken down into component parts, or expanded. You may wish to add a section for gathering information about the respondent: grade level, academic program, and such. For younger children, parts of this survey can be used as the basis of an interview.

Student Library Survey

1. Have you used the library this year?
______ Yes (Go to question 7 and continue)
______ No (Answer questions 2–6 only)

2. What is the reason why you have not used the library?

______ a. The library is not open when I can go there.

______ b. There is nothing there that interests me.

______ c. I do not have assignments that make me use the library.

______ d. I use another library.

______ e. I use resources I have at home.

3. If you use other libraries, which ones do you use? (check all that apply)

______ a. Public library

______ b. College library

______ c. Other (please name) ___________________________________

4. If you use resources at home, which ones do you use? (Rank in order of frequency, 1 = most often; 3 = least often.)

______ a. Internet

______ b. Magazines

______ c. Books

5. If you use other libraries or home resources, why? (Rank in order of importance, 1 = most important; 5 = least important.)

______ I need books the school library does not own.

______ I find other libraries easier to use.

______ I do not have time during the school day to use the library.

______ My Internet is faster at home.

______ Other (please explain)

6. Finish this sentence: I would visit the library more if _________________.

7. How often do you use the library?

______ a. Every day

______ b. A few times a week

______ c. Once a week

______ d. A few times per marking period

______ e. A few times per year

8. When I go to the library, I usually do the following (check all that apply)

______ a. Find books or other materials for pleasure and personal interests

______ b. Get information for reports or projects

______ d. Use computers

______ e. Read magazines

10. Please rate the library's physical environment in the following areas:

Seating	Excellent	Very Good	Average	Fair	Poor
Lighting	Excellent	Very Good	Average	Fair	Poor
Temperature	Excellent	Very Good	Average	Fair	Poor
Noise level	Excellent	Very Good	Average	Fair	Poor
Signs	Excellent	Very Good	Average	Fair	Poor
Cleanliness	Excellent	Very Good	Average	Fair	Poor
Furniture	Excellent	Very Good	Average	Fair	Poor

11. Please rate the library's educational programs in the following areas:

Librarian's attitude	Excellent	Very Good	Average	Fair	Poor
Staff members' attitudes	Excellent	Very Good	Average	Fair	Poor
Individual help	Excellent	Very Good	Average	Fair	Poor
Small group help	Excellent	Very Good	Average	Fair	Poor
Classes taught	Excellent	Very Good	Average	Fair	Poor

12. How would you judge your ability in using the information resources of the library?

_____ a. Excellent

_____ b. Very good

_____ c. Average

_____ d. Fair

_____ e. Poor

13. Overall, how satisfied are you with the services of the library?

_____ a. Very dissatisfied

_____ b. Dissatisfied

_____ c. Slightly dissatisfied

_____ d. Slightly satisfied

_____ e. Satisfied

_____ f. Very satisfied

14. What is your favorite thing about the library?

15. What one service or function would you like the library to improve or change? Please describe how the library might do this.

Surveys like the preceding one can be distributed electronically using online survey tools. These tools can be inexpensive (e.g., Survey Monkey) or free (e.g., Google Forms). New tools and apps are constantly being developed. Plickers is an app that school librarians can use to poll their class for free, without the need for student devices. Students use paper cards which are scanned with an iPhone/iPad for instant checks-for-understanding, exit tickets, and impromptu polls (Educational Technology and Mobile Learning 2018).

LIBRARY ATTENDANCE

The most effortless way to count library attendance is with an automatic turnstile. However, these are uncommon in a school library setting. There are several alternatives:

- Use a manual clicker and assign an aide or clerk to count students as they come in the door.
- Have a library sign-in sheet to record attendance. Break it down by grade or purpose for further detailed analysis.
- Use Google Sheets for electronic sign-in. Interesting graphs can be constructed.
- If passes are used, save them.
- Count all students in the library whether they are there individually or with a class.

A count of library attendance for one typical day can yield myriad interesting statistics:

$$\textbf{Attendance per hour} = \frac{\text{attendance per day}}{\text{number of hours library is open}}$$

$$\textbf{Attendance per week} = \text{attendance per day} \times 5$$
$$\textbf{Attendance per month} = (\text{attendance per day}) \times (\text{days per month})$$
$$\textbf{Attendance per year} = (\text{attendance per day}) \times (\text{days per year})$$

$$\textbf{Visits per student} = \frac{\text{attendance per year}}{\text{total number of students}}$$

One does not need to track attendance every day and every period. Choose a typical week or sample just one random day per week and extrapolate the results.

Statistics taken from the *Iowa School Library Study: School Level Results* (Hanover Research 2016) can be applied to your library attendance for comparison. Table 5.1 shows the percentage of the total student population of the school visiting the library during a week for independent reading, research, or study that is not part of a scheduled class. It also shows the percentage of the total student population of the school visiting the library during a week

Table 5-1 Percentage of Students Visiting the School Library during a Typical Week

	0%–25%		26%–50%		51%–75%		76%–99%		100%	
	V	S	V	S	V	S	V	S	V	S
Elementary	49%	4%	24%	6%	15%	6%	9%	16%	4%	68%
Middle	23%	24%	41%	33%	28%	22%	8%	16%	1%	5%
High	41%	44%	42%	41%	9%	12%	7%	1%	1%	2%

V = Voluntarily choose to come to the library
S = Scheduled as part of a class
Source: Iowa School Library Study: School Level Results 2016

for planned, scheduled instruction on information literacy skills or for other curriculum work. This includes any students who visited the library with a group or class, including classes visiting the library for book checkout. This does not include students who visited the library voluntarily.

SCHOOL LIBRARIANS' EVALUATION OF STUDENTS

Student Behavior

"Student achievement at the end of the year is directly related to the degree to which the teacher establishes good control of the classroom procedures in the very first week of the school year" (Wong and Wong 2018, 6). By establishing expectations and consistently adhering to routines and procedures, learning can take place. The school library is slightly different from the classroom in regard to procedures (Pentland 2018; Weisburg and Toor 2015). Use the list in table 5.2 to check whether you have the routines in place that will foster success.

Table 5-2 Typical School Library Routines, Procedures, and Expectations

Check the appropriate box

Yes	No	In Progress	
☐	☐	☐	First few minutes a class comes into the library
☐	☐	☐	Check out and check in
☐	☐	☐	Coming to the library as an individual from a classroom or study hall
☐	☐	☐	Quieting a class
☐	☐	☐	Dismissal
☐	☐	☐	Voice levels

Continued

Table 5-2   Continued

Yes	No	In Progress	
☐	☐	☐	Lunch policy
☐	☐	☐	Makerspace usage
☐	☐	☐	Computer usage
☐	☐	☐	Lost books
☐	☐	☐	Overdue books
☐	☐	☐	Rules for behavior
☐	☐	☐	Acceptable use policy
☐	☐	☐	Bathroom rules (if not in the library)
☐	☐	☐	Mobile devices (if not a school-wide policy)

EVALUATING STUDENT LEARNING OUTCOMES

School librarians as true instructional partners not only coplan and coteach but also coassess students. "Unless they participate in assessment, school librarians will be unable to collect evidence of the effectiveness of their teaching. They will lack the data they need to adjust their instruction in order to improve student learning outcomes. School librarians who want to be considered equals with classroom teacher colleagues will assess students' learning and use the resulting data to inform their teaching" (Moreillon 2018, 118).

Rubrics

Formative assessment tasks are frequently evaluated by scoring devices called *assessment matrices* or *rubrics*. Rubrics can be simple or detailed, depending on the complexity of the task and the desired competencies to be achieved. Most teachers use rubrics, and students are used to them. Rubrics can be developed independently or modified from existing resources (Schrock 2019).

Rubistar (4teachers 2020) is one of those tools. One can use the preloaded templates to create rubrics in all subject areas by choosing a topic (such as oral projects), a subcategory (such as class debate), and the related scoring categories. For class debate, the categories are respect for other team, information, rebuttal, use of facts/statistics, presentation style, organization, and understanding of topic. Once the desired categories are chosen, the rubric self-generates with wording developed in four levels. There are options to change text and rename categories (http://rubistar.4teachers.org/index.php).

Exit Tickets

Exit tickets are a worthwhile formative assessment technique for school librarians who do not see the same students on a regular basis. Exit tickets provide answers to a question or prompt that is asked of all students at the end of a class. Each student writes their answer on a small piece of paper, Post-it note, or specially designed printable (figure 5.1), and they turn them in as they exit. Various apps and programs enable the creation and implementation of digital exit tickets as well (Miller 2019). Stewart (2015) describes the "parking lot" technique for exit tickets:

> One method for the parking lot is to wait until almost the end of class and have students write their success and struggles on a sticky note. As the students are dismissed from class, they place their exit ticket on the poster. The other method is for students to jot down any questions they have on a sticky note, and place on the poster before the end of class. If time allows, you can address a few of the exit tickets before the class leaves. Hint: have students write their initials on the paper so that you know how to direct your instruction to assist them.

Some examples of questions/prompts are the following:

- One thing I learned ____
- I have a question about ____
- What from today's lesson will you try to apply to your learning? What was helpful?
- What was a struggle to understand?
- What do you think you would be able to teach to your classmates? What was confusing?
- What was the theme of the story?
- I would like to learn more about _________________ (Stewart 2015)

The exit ticket can be used to plan instruction as you gain an understanding of who knows what and whether certain subjects need additional instruction time. This enables grouping students in teams the next day based on their answers, with one of the students in each team having a good grasp of the solution or answer (Goodrich 2012). Exit tickets, as evidence of comprehension, are powerful assessment pieces for student portfolios (Renwick 2017).

OTHER CONSIDERATIONS REGARDING STUDENTS

Library Privacy

Protecting user privacy and confidentiality is a basic tenet of librarianship. A profusion of data on students can be gathered in a typical school library

EXIT TICKET

One thing I learned is . . .

But I still have a question about . . .

I would like to learn more about . . .

Figure 5.1   Sample exit ticket

based on the resources they access, collections they use, and the questions they ask. The American Library Association (ALA 2006) recommends the following:

> School librarians should conduct privacy audits to determine the current threats to student privacy and what protections are already in place. The audit should cover the library management system; computer and network use in the library; eBooks and other online content; interactive Web tools; social media; and other technologies such as scanners/photocopiers and surveillance cameras. The results of the audit can be used to help create or revise privacy policies.

In that regard, ALA has developed a checklist (figure 5.2) intended to help libraries implement the principles laid out in the "Library Privacy Guidelines for Students in K–12 Schools."

SPECIAL POPULATIONS

Lesbian, Gay, Bisexual, Transgender, and Queer (LGBTQ)

School libraries can often play an important role for LGBTQ students looking to find information about coming out, health issues, and family topics as well as recreational reading. LGBTQ students also seek refuge in the school library for safety and to avoid being bullied. Various researchers and professional groups have addressed various aspects of LGBTQ school library services, which include access (Rubin 1995; Winerip 2012), collections (Hughes-Hassell, Overberg, and Harris 2013), and beliefs and attitudes (National Alliance to End Homelessness et al. 2009; Perez 2019). Based on these findings, use the following worksheet (table 5.3) to indicate your level of attentiveness to these issues.

Autism

Over the past two decades, the prevalence of autism spectrum disorder (ASD) has risen significantly and is currently the fastest-growing disability in the United States. The most recent report from the Centers for Disease Control and Prevention (2019) confirms that it is present in approximately one child in every fifty-nine. A multiyear research project at Florida State University has compiled an implementation guide for librarians to serve this population (Everhart, Woods, and Anderson 2018), and various aspects of the guide have been provided to evaluate responsiveness to students with ASD's needs (table 5.4). Addressing concerns of this special population will make the school library more conducive to all students.

Priority 1 Actions

_____ 1. Create internal library procedures to protect student privacy based on:
    _____ a. School policies related to privacy and confidentiality of student data, especially student circulation records and the use of library resources in all formats.
    _____ b. Federal laws such as the Family Educational Rights and Privacy Act (FERPA), Children's Online Privacy Protection Act (COPPA), and state privacy laws regarding library records.
    _____ c. ALA and AASL policy statements, online tool kits and Q & A's, guidelines, and other resources provided by national and state library associations.
_____ 2. Collect the minimum amount of information necessary about students to conduct library business.
_____ 3. Configure circulation software to delete students' borrowing history and retain only necessary records.
_____ 4. Ensure any paper records with sensitive information are stored in a secure area and shredded when no longer needed.
_____ 5. Train library staff and volunteers to respect students' privacy and the confidentiality of their library records.

Priority 2 Actions

_____ 1. Educate administrators, faculty, and support staff about students' library privacy and the confidentiality of student data using a variety of communication methods.
    _____ a. Initiate conversations with the principal, teachers, students, and parents about the need for an official library privacy policy.
_____ 2. Add privacy-related resources to the library collection including items related to personal privacy, minors' privacy rights, and privacy as a national and international issue.
    _____ a. Consider creating a privacy information section on the school library web page or a privacy-themed pathfinder (e.g., LibGuide) with privacy resources.
_____ 3. Integrate online privacy into library instruction and programming. For example:
    _____ a. Introduce students to online privacy information such as secure passwords and web tracking during library orientations and other brief presentations.
    _____ b. Celebrate Choose Privacy Week and other privacy-related observances (Data Privacy Day, Teen Tech Week, etc.) with the school community.
    _____ c. Create privacy-related displays and set up videos in the library to educate parents during parent-teacher conferences and other evening school and community events
    _____ d. Offer presentations to parents about students' privacy online and other topics of interest to families.
_____ 4. Advocate within the school or district for protecting students' privacy rights in learning management systems or other technologies that enable educators to monitor student reading and research habits. Assessment should not include monitoring how students use specific library materials and online resources as part of free inquiry and research.
_____ 5. Volunteer to serve on the school's data governance committee. If one does not exist, advocate for its creation.

Priority 3 Actions

_____ 1. Work with other stakeholders in the school or district to create an official library privacy policy in regards to student circulation records and the use of library resources.
    _____ a. The privacy policy should be approved by the school's governing body (e.g., school board, school committee, etc.)
    _____ b. Post the policy in the library and on the library's section of the school website.
    _____ c. Promote the library's privacy policy within the school community.
_____ 2. Work through school lines of authority to write or adapt a K-12 privacy curriculum and have it formally approved and taught. Collaboratively teach privacy units with teachers using the iKEEPSAFE and/or other privacy curricula.
_____ 3. Work with school officials to incorporate privacy protections into RFP's and resulting contracts. Discuss privacy concerns with digital resource and technology vendors, especially in regards to the school's/library's contracts with these vendors.
_____ 4. Ensure that all online transactions between client applications and server applications are encrypted.
_____ 5. Ensure that storage of personally identifiable student information is housed using encrypted storage.

Figure 5.2 Library Privacy Checklist for Students in K-12 Schools

Source: "Library Privacy Checklist for Students in K-12 Schools," American Library Association, February 6, 2017. http://www.ala.org/advocacy/privacy/checklists/students (Accessed December 10, 2019). Developed by the Intellectual Freedom Committee of the American Library Association.

130

Table 5-3   Survey of Responsiveness to Serving LGBTQ Students

What I do about . . .

Access	Very Little				Very Much
Are books directly available for students to check out or are they available by "staff recommendation" or parental permission only?	1	2	3	4	5
Are books separated, self-contained, or labeled or integrated with the rest of the collection?	1	2	3	4	5
Are websites to information about the LGBTQ community blocked?	1	2	3	4	5

Collection					
LGBTQ books are contained in both fiction and nonfiction.	1	2	3	4	5
LGBTQ titles are on reading lists.	1	2	3	4	5
LGBTQ titles are used in displays.	1	2	3	4	5
LGBTQ titles are used in booktalks or storytimes.	1	2	3	4	5
LGBTQ titles are recommended to teachers for inclusion in the curriculum.	1	2	3	4	5
Weed out books that categorize homosexuality as a mental health issue, that are otherwise discriminatory, or that contain outdated material.	1	2	3	4	5

Beliefs and Attitudes					
Be able to use the words *gay*, *lesbian*, *bisexual*, and *transgender* appropriately when talking with youth, other employees, and volunteers.	1	2	3	4	5
Call students by their preferred first name and pronoun in accordance with their gender identity or expression.	1	2	3	4	5
Know what to do when a student self-discloses his or her sexual or gender identity (e.g., offer support, engage in conversation if youth wants to, maintain privacy, and locate appropriate services and support for the student).	1	2	3	4	5
Prevent harassment and discrimination by valuing and affirming differences and appropriately responding to verbal, emotional, and physical threats against any student.	1	2	3	4	5
Ensure that staff do not disclose a student's sexual orientation or gender identity.	1	2	3	4	5
Read, be seen reading, and talk about books with LGBTQ voices.	1	2	3	4	5

Table 5-4 Survey of Responsiveness to Serving Students with Autism

What I do about . . .

Communication and Social Interaction	**Very Little**			**Very Much**	
Share attention on an object rather than forcing eye contact.	1	2	3	4	5
Be very direct by explain feelings and directions, as social cues and body language may not be understood.	1	2	3	4	5
Speak literally and avoid the use of sarcasm, metaphors, idioms, and irony.	1	2	3	4	5
Alert students to any transitions.	1	2	3	4	5
Ask direct rather than open-ended questions during a reference interview.	1	2	3	4	5
Encourage communicative interaction in a common area where louder vocal volume will not be a concern, but always ensure the availability of a safe "break space" whenever possible.	1	2	3	4	5
Offer alternative ways to communicate, such as through drawing or using an iPad.	1	2	3	4	5
Use a polite statement in lieu of a question. For example, "Tell me more about your assignment, and I will help you."	1	2	3	4	5

Environment					
Fluorescent lights are eliminated as much as possible.	1	2	3	4	5
Signs are clear and consistent.	1	2	3	4	5
Quiet study rooms, pods, or individual study areas are available.	1	2	3	4	5
Rugs keep sound to a minimum.	1	2	3	4	5
Fidget tools are available to self-regulate behavior.	1	2	3	4	5
Visual boundaries clearly define spaces.	1	2	3	4	5

Technology					
Allow for self-checkout.	1	2	3	4	5
Have noise-canceling headphones for checkout.	1	2	3	4	5
Foster fixed interests by demonstrating how to find and access any of the available online tools for creating photo galleries, comic strips, and journals.	1	2	3	4	5
Check your library's website for accessibility.	1	2	3	4	5
Educate parents about Internet safety.	1	2	3	4	5

1. In what year did you graduate from (name of school)?
   - ○ 2017
   - ○ 2018
   - ○ 2019
2. What grades did you attend (name of school)?
   - ○ 5th grade
   - ○ 6th grade
   - ○ 7th grade
   - ○ 8th grade
   - ○ 9th grade
   - ○ 10th grade
   - ○ 11th grade
   - ○ 12th grade
3. Have you had to write papers in college that required research?
   - ○ Yes
   - ○ No
4. Approximately how many papers are you asked to write each semester?
   - ○ 1-3
   - ○ 4-6
   - ○ 7-10
5. In what college courses were you asked to write research papers?

6. What citation style were you asked to use?
   - ○ MLA
   - ○ Chicago
   - ○ APA
   - ○ Other:
7. What citation tools do you use?
   - ○ Noodletools
   - ○ RefWorks
   - ○ Zotero
   - ○ EasyBib
   - ○ Endnote
   - ○ Other: _______________________________

Figure 5.3   Graduate Library Survey
Reprinted with permission of Cathy Evans, Director of Libraries at St. Mary's Episcopal School, Memphis, Tennessee.

8. What type of sources did you use to write your college papers?
   - ○ Print books
   - ○ E-books
   - ○ Magazines
   - ○ Scholarly Journals
   - ○ Websites
   - ○ Other: _________________________________

9. What databases did you find most useful in writing your college papers?

10. Was any type of assistance or instruction offered by the college?
   - ○ Yes
   - ○ No

11. If assistance or instruction was offered, who provided the assistance?
   - ○ Instructor
   - ○ Librarian
   - ○ Writing lab
   - ○ Online tutorials
   - ○ Other:_________________________________

12. Was plagiarism ever discussed in your college classes? (more than a mere mention)
   - ○ Yes
   - ○ No

Reflecting upon the learning and experiences you had at (name of school) answer the following:

13. How confident did you feel in your understanding of plagiarism?
   - ○ Very
   - ○ Somewhat
   - ○ Not at all

14. How confident did you feel in your understanding of how to avoid plagiarism?
   - ○ Very
   - ○ Somewhat
   - ○ Not at all

Figure 5.3 Continued

15. How confident did you feel in your ability to cite your sources?

   ○ Very

   ○ Somewhat

   ○ Not at all

16. How confident did you feel in your ability to find quality sources for your papers?

   ○ Very

   ○ Somewhat

   ○ Not at all

17. How confident did you feel in your ability to develop a good thesis for your papers?

   ○ Very

   ○ Somewhat

   ○ Not at all

18. How confident did you feel in your ability to effectively use and integrate your sources in your papers?

   ○ Very

   ○ Somewhat

   ○ Not at all

19. How confident did you feel in your ability to use your college library?

   ○ Very

   ○ Somewhat

   ○ Not at all

   ○ Other: ____

20. Is there an area or aspect of the college paper process that you wish you had known more about?

21. Overall how would you rate your readiness to write college level papers

   ○ Excellent

   ○ Good

   ○ Fair

   ○ Poor

22. Any other feedback you would like to give the librarians so that we might improve what we do to prepare our graduates for college level research?

Figure 5.3 Continued

Alumni

Another method to gauge a school library program's success is to determine how well it prepares its graduates. A survey developed by Evans (2016) shown in figure 5.3 has been used to assess the impact of the school library program on how well alumni navigate writing papers, citing sources, and addressing plagiarism in college. Surveying those with firsthand knowledge serves the following purposes:

- Provide better understanding of the effectiveness of the school library experience;
- Be used for program improvement;
- Highlight what the program is doing well; and
- Educate stakeholders (parents, administrators, community) about how well a school prepares its graduates. (Gulla and Jorgenson 2014)

REFERENCES

American Library Association. 2016. "Library Privacy Checklist for Students in K–12 Schools." Last modified May 5. http://www.ala.org /advocacy/privacy/guidelines/students.

Centers for Disease Control and Prevention. 2019. "Data & Statistics on Autism Spectrum Disorder." Last modified April 5. https://www.cdc .gov/ncbddd/autism/data.html.

Educational Technology and Mobile Learning. 2018. "17 of the Best Surveys and Polls Creation Tools for Teachers and Educators," *Education Technology and Mobile Learning* (blog), February 28. https://www.edu catorstechnology.com/2018/02/17-of-best-surveys-and-polls-creation .html.

Evans, Cathy. 2016. "Notes from the Field: Assessing the Impact of Our Library Program." *School Library Connection* 45 (2): 28.

Everhart, Nancy, Juliann Woods, and Amelia Anderson. 2018. "Project A+: Serving Students with Autism Spectrum Disorder in the Academic Library." http://purl.flvc.org/fsu/fd/FSU_libsubv1_scholarship_submission _1524754052_db70ce00.

Goodrich, Kelly. 2012. "Classroom Techniques: Formative Assessment Idea Number Two." *Teach Learn Grow* (blog), NWEA, September 5. https://www.nwea.org/blog/2012/classroom-techniques-formative -assessment-idea-number-two.

Gulla, John, and Olaf Jorgenson. 2014. "Measuring Our Success: How to Gauge the 'Value Added' by an Independent School Education." *Independent School* 73 (3). ERIC (EJ1048092). https://www.nais.org/magazine /independent-school/spring-2014/measuring-our-success/.

Hanover Research. 2016. *Iowa School Library Study: School Level Results*. 2016. Arlington: Hanover Research. https://educateiowa.gov/sites/files /ed/documents/2015-2016IowaSchoolLibraryStudy-SchoolLevels -Heartland%20AEA.pdf.

Hughes-Hassell, Sandra, Elizabeth Overberg, and Shannon Harris. 2013. "Lesbian, Gay, Bisexual, Transgender, and Questioning (LGBTQ)– Themed Literature for Teens: Are School Libraries Providing Adequate Collections?" *School Library Research* 16: 1–18. http://www.ala.org /aasl/sites/ala.org.aasl/files/content/aaslpubsandjournals/slr/vol16/SLR _LGBTQThemedLiteratureforTeens_V16.pdf.

Miller, Matt. 2019. "10 Ideas for Digital Exit Tickets (and Some Analog Ones, Too)." *Ditch That Textbook* (blog), March 27. http://ditchthattext book.com/2019/03/27/10-ideas-for-digital-exit-tickets-and-some -analog-ones-too.

Moreillon, Judi. 2018. *Maximizing School Librarian Leadership: Building Connections for Learning and Advocacy*. Chicago: ALA Editions.

National Alliance to End Homelessness, National Network for Youth, Lambda Legal, and the National Center for Lesbian Rights. 2009. "National Recommended Best Practices for Serving LGBT Homeless Youth." Lambda Legal, April 20. https://www.lambdalegal.org/publications /national-recommended-best-practices-for-lgbt-homeless-youth.

Pentland, Courtney. 2018. "Classroom Management in the School Library." *Teacher Librarian* 45 (4): 34–37. Academic OneFile (edsgcl.537982252).

Perez, Vanessa. 2019. "Libraries Can Be LGBTQ-Affirming Spaces on School Campuses." *Literacy & NTCE* (blog), National Council of Teachers of English, February 28. https://www2.ncte.org/blog/2019/02 /libraries-can-be-lgbtq-affirming-spaces-on-school-campuses.

Renwick, Matt. 2017. *Digital Portfolios in the Classroom: Showcasing and Assessing Student Work*. Alexandria, VA: ASCD. eBook Collection, EBSCOhost (1590963).

Rubin, Steven A. 1995. "Children Who Grow Up with Gay or Lesbian Parents: How Are Today's Schools Meeting This 'Invisible' Group's Needs?" PhD diss., University of Wisconsin-Madison. ERIC (ED386290).

Schrock, Kathy. 2019. "Assessment and Rubrics." *Kathy Schrock's Guide to Everything.* Last modified March 28. https://www.schrockguide.net /assessment-and-rubrics.html.

Stewart, Rhonda. 2015. "Using Exit Tickets as an Assessment Tool." *Top Teaching Blog, Scholastic*, March 13. https://www.scholastic.com /teachers/blog-posts/rhonda-stewart/using-exit-tickets-assessment-tool.

Weisburg, Hilda K., and Ruth Toor. 2015. *New on the Job: A School Librarian's Guide to Success.* 2nd ed. Chicago: ALA Editions.

Winerip, Michael. 2012. "Missouri School District Questioned over Anti-Gay Web Filter." *New York Times*, March 26. https://www.nytimes .com/2012/03/26/education/missouri-school-district-questioned-over -anti-gay-web-filter.html.

Wong, Harry K., and Rosemary T. Wong. 2018. *The First Days of School: How to Be an Effective Teacher.* 5th ed. Mountain View, CA: Harry K. Wong Publications.

Chapter 6
Curriculum

Curriculum involvement of the school librarian is crucial, but also confusing. Several studies over the years have acknowledged that practicing school librarians, despite recommendations from national guidelines, have been reluctant to take on this role (Merga 2019; Everhart, Mardis, and Johnston 2011). Much of this reluctance stems from a lack of knowledge about where information literacy "fits" in the curriculum and the strategies required to fully plan, execute, and evaluate instruction. Furthermore, there is ambiguity as to the delineation of responsibilities with classroom teachers in the process of implementing cooperative units and lessons. Weisburg and Toor (2015) encourage new school librarians to become members of their school's curriculum committee to become familiar with what is being taught and to demonstrate their value in locating information outside the district to complement units.

The checklist in figure 6.1 enables you to self-assess your knowledge of your school's curriculum (Sherrington 2019; Danielson Group 2013; Everhart, Mardis, and Johnston 2011). It can be used to bring into focus areas where you may need to obtain more information that will enhance your curricular role.

Curriculum maps are excellent visual tools to learn about what is being taught in the school. The map displays in spreadsheet form how standards, grade levels, subjects, skills, and resources relate to each other. Individual teachers, including the school librarian, may develop a scope and sequence for their grade level or subject. A scope and sequence is often a starting

	Aware	Unaware	Need to find out more	Not applicable
1. School-wide initiatives				
State standards				
Data for decision making				
SMART goals or other standard goals/objectives				
Required lesson plan form				
Standard rubric format				
Questioning techniques				
Citation format				
Kindness/ethics initiatives				
Heterogeneous/homogeneous grouping				
Integration of technology				
Writing/reading across the curriculum				
School-wide special events				
Textbooks and/or open educational resources				
2. Student achievement				
Standardized tests				
Honors courses				
Grading scheme				
Teacher exams and assessments				
3. Subjects and grade levels				
Big ideas that are covered				
Core curriculum for all students				
Major projects currently utilizing the library				
Major projects that could potentially be utilizing the library				
Periods of history that are covered				
Controversial topics that are covered				
Electives				
Curriculum for students with special needs or gifted				
Online courses				
Knowledge of master schedule				

Figure 6.1 Knowledge of School Curriculum Checklist

4. Reading				
Works of literature that are read in classrooms				
Classroom required reading lists				
Summer reading lists				
Reading management programs				
5. Teachers				
Who is responsible for grades/subjects				
Teacher incentives				
Evaluation framework for teachers				
Teams and committees				
Learning communities				
Opportunities for growth and development				

Figure 6.1 Continued

point for a curriculum map because it illustrates when skills will be taught and the order they will be taught, as shown in figure 6.2.

Curriculum mapping takes the scope and sequence a step further and helps answer the question of where information literacy should be placed in the curriculum as a whole. It leads to a more comprehensive and sequential information literacy program that is better integrated into the institution (Archambault and Masunaga 2015).

COLLABORATION WITH TEACHERS

Involvement in the curriculum naturally leads to opportunities for collaboration with teachers. However, not all forms of collaboration are equal. In figure 6.3, Loertscher (2000) describes the various levels of school librarian and teacher collaboration.

The output measures devised by Bradburn (1999) are another approach to evaluating planning and teaching. Calculating and retaining these statistics can be a powerful technique to inform administrators of lost opportunities due to overscheduling, fixed scheduling, or lack of clerical help.

$$\textbf{Planning Opportunity Rate} = 100\% - \frac{\text{\# modified or unfilled planning requests}}{\text{\# planning requests received from teachers}}$$

$$\textbf{Teaching Availability Rate} = 100\% - \frac{\text{\# modified or unfilled teaching requests}}{\text{\# teaching requests received from teachers}}$$

2018-2019 Media Center Scope and Sequence

1st Nine Weeks

Week of	Kindergarten	1st Grade	2nd Grade	3rd Grade	4th Grade	5th Grade
August 13			Orientations and first check outs			
August 20			Checkout Only- No lessons			
August 27	Book Fair					
September 3 (Sept 3- Labor Day)			Checkout Only- No lessons Pull books for Hp Reveal Book Hunt			
September 10 (Sept 14- Dot Day)	Orientation MC Rules/Manners		How to Meet Your AR Goals with Big Universe Review Good Fit Books/AR labels and bookmarks	Checkout Only-No lessons		
September 17	Review MC Rules and Book Care Watch Book Care Video Practice Library Book		Checkout Only-No lessons		Using Destiny Fiction Hunt w/Hp REveal Or NF Hunt with QR codes	
September 24	How to check out a book Book Care worksheet review Begin checkout		What are genres? Realistic Fiction	Using Destiny With Chromebooks	Checkout Only-No lessons	
October 1 (Oct 4- MS Consortium, 5- Work Day)	Fiction Read There Was an Old Lady Who Swallowed some Leaves Complete worksheet about fiction		Fantasy/SF	Checkout Only-No lessons		
October 8 (October 8-Fall Break)	Non-fiction Read The Zieglers and Their Apple Orchard Complete non-fiction worksheet		Checkout Only-No lessons			

Figure 6.2   Library media center scope and sequence

Source: Reprinted with permission from Jo Nase, Media Specialist, A Teacher's Bag of Tricks/The Book Bug

2nd Nine Weeks

Week of	PreK	Kindergarten	1st Grade	2nd Grade	3rd Grade	4th Grade	5th Grade
October 15		Read *The Mouse and the Apple* Complete Worksheet		Mystery	Internet Safety and Manners (Chromebooks)	Checkout Only- No lessons	
October 22 GMAS field test 23-26		Read *The Little Old Lady Who Was Not Afraid of Anything* Discuss characters, theme and plot Complete activity sheet reviewing these story elements terms	Checking out books from the BIG shelves Read *We're Going on a Book Hunt*	Checkout Only- No lessons		Internet Safety and Manners (Chromebooks)	
October 29	By the Light of the Harvest Moon	Review Book Care Read *Never Let a Ghost Borrow Your Library Book* Complete Book Care worksheet		Historical Fiction	**Dictionary Dude** (Chromebooks)	Checkout Only-No lessons	
November 5 GaETC 7-9	One Little, Two Little, Three Little Pilgrims	Book Care Review, Cont'd Read Penelope Popper Book Doctor		Checkout Only-No lessons (Pull books for Traditional Literature lesson)			
November 12	*Twas the Night Before Thanksgiving*	Story elements Read *Twas the Night Before Thanksgiving*		Checkout Only-No lessons		Search Engines and Types of Searches (Chromebooks)	
November 19		Thanksgiving Break					
November 26	*The Night Before the Night Before Christmas*	Five Finger Rule Read *Goldie Socks and the Three Libearians* Just Right Book worksheet (Those first graders that are ready for chapter books- move up)		Traditional Literature with Genre Detective Activity	**Encyclopedia PPT** What subject do I look up? (Chromebooks)	Checkout Only-No lessons	
December 3	*How Santa Got His Job*	Review story elements How Santa Got His Job		Checkout Only-No lessons		Note Taking Practice /Partner research of famous American (Chromebooks)	
December 10	Reading Tent/Inventory						
December 17	Reading Tent/Inventory						

Figure 6.2 Continued

3rd Nine Weeks

Week of	PreK	Kindergarten	1st Grade	2nd Grade	3rd Grade	4th Grade	5th Grade
January 1 (students-Jan 4)		Checkout Only-No lessons					
January 7	*There Was Cold Lady Who Swallowed Some Snow*	Read *Squirrel's New Year's Resolution* and review book care With the Library Ninja PowerPoint (Begin Practice Shelves with K)		Checkout Only-No lessons		New Years Resolutions (taking care of books) Discover Your Genre	
January 14 (Jan 17 MS Consortium)	*Happy Birthday, MLK*	*Biography* *Happy Birthday, MLK*		New Years Resolutions Dewey Body Buddy Non-fiction hunt w/Non-fiction helper	Atlases (Chromebooks)	Checkout Only- No lessons	
January 21 MLK Jan 21	*Pat the Penguin*	*Pat the Penguin* on Epic! Books Quiver with Penguin Page	Read *Miss Brooks Loves Books and I Don't* Move up students to big shelves as needed basis on STAR scores	Checkout Only- No lessons			
January 28		Book Fair Video (BF Set up Jan 31/ Preview Feb 1)		Checkout Only-No lessons			
February 4		Book Fair- Kick off of Love to Read Month					
February 11	Be A Friend	Kindness Week Read Be A Friend Complete Kindness Sheet		Book Awards/ Love to Read Month Centers		Checkout Only-No lessons	
February 18		Mid-Winter Break					
February 25	You Are (Not) Small	Read Lion Lessons Make lion craft or discuss story elements	Read *Alpha Betti* ABC order and Shelf Order	Checkout Only-No lessons		Book Awards/ Love to Read Month Centers	
March 4	We Are Growing	Read *Miss Brooks Loves Books and I Don't* Emily Arrow's song *Books* Talk about what makes a book " just right."	Women's History Month Read biographies Eleanor Roosevelt and Marian Anderson	Checkout Only-No lessons			
March 11	*The Night Before St. Patrick's Day*	Story Elements: *The Night Before St. Patrick's Day* Use HP Reveal with iPad		Genredy or Genre Detective Activity (review of Genres)	Research/ Reference Review (chromebooks)	Checkout Only-No lessons	

© 2019 ATBOT/ The Book Bug

Figure 6.2 Continued

4th Nine Weeks

Week of	Pre K	Kindergarten	1st Grade	2nd Grade	3rd Grade	4th Grade	5th Grade
March 18 March 20th PreK Lottery	Lion Lessons	Checking out books from the BIG shelves Read *We're Going on a Book Hunt*	Guidance Lesson with Veal Checkout afterwards	Checkout Only-No lessons		Research/ Reference Review (chromebooks)	
March 25 March 29th Career Day 8-11	Read *In My Garden* and *Plants in Spring* On Epic!	Read *In My Garden* and *Plants in Spring* On Epic!	No lesson or checkout due to testing in the Media Center	Checkout Only-No lessons			
April 1	Spring Break						
April 8 National Library Week Testing begins on Wednesday	Do Not Bring Your Dragon to the Library or Community Helper: Librarians	Milestones Testing// Checkout Only, after testing is complete					
April 15		Milestones Testing// Checkout Only- after testing is complete					
April 22 Earth Day April 25 Poem in Your Pocket Day	Read Earth Day book On Epic!	Earth Day book and activity Read Earth Day book On Epic!	Non-fiction: *Owl book (on Epic!)* Introduce BIG Non-fiction section Move all students up to the E section	Checkout Only-No lessons		MakerSpaces/ Summer Reading Opportunities	
April 29	Mother's Day Books or The Thank You Book	MakerSpaces (Osmo Tangrams, Monster, Words, Numbers,)		MakerSpaces/ Summer Reading Opportunities		Checkout Only	
May 6 Teacher Appreciation Week Last day for checkout May 8 Set up Book Fair May 9	Set up Book Fair	Summer Reading Opportunities Or The Thank You book Mother's Day Flipgrid/ music video Or Library Memory Book		Checkout Only			
May 13		BOGO Book Fair/Inventory					
May 20-25 Red Carpet Reader Celebration May 20		Inventory					

© 2019 ATBOT/ The Book Bug

Figure 6.2 Continued

	Librarian's Taxonomy	**Teacher's Taxonomy**
Level 1	No involvement. Library media center is bypassed.	No involvement of library media center specialist or use of materials from the library media center.
Level 2	Students access information when needed.	Permanent room collection created. Little need to interact with the library media center.
Level 3	Specific requests from teachers and students addressed.	Materials borrowed from the library media center, public library, or other sources for classroom use.
Level 4	Materials gathered on the spur of the moment.	Library media center specialist provides ideas and suggestions regarding materials for instruction.
Level 5	Informal planning in hall or lunchroom.	Use of library media center materials to supplement unit content.
Level 6	Advance notice for needed library materials.	Library media center materials/activities are integral to unit content rather than supplementary.
Level 7	A concerted effort to promote library.	Library media specialist is a teaching partner to construct unit of instruction (of information literacy).
Level 8	Formal planning with teacher on a resource-based project or unit.	Library media specialist is consulted as curriculum changes are being considered.
*Level 9	Participation in development, execution, and evaluation of a resource-based teaching unit (Level 1).	
*Level 10	Participation in resource-based teaching units where the entire unit content depends on the resources of the LMC program (Level 11).	
Level 11	Participation and contribution made along with teachers to planning and structure of what will be taught in school.	

Figure 6.3 Loertscher's taxonomy

Source: Based on David V. Loertscher. 2000. *Taxonomies of the School Library Media Program*. 2nd Ed. San Jose, CA: Hi Willow Research & Pub.

	Exemplary	Proficient	Needs Improvement
Collaboration exists between the library professional staff and more than 50 percent of the classroom teachers.			
The library media program is an integral, essential component of the school's instructional program.			
The classroom teachers and the library professional staff work together as an instructional team to plan and implement learning activities that incorporate information literacy and technology skills as an integral part of the curriculum.			
The classroom teachers and the library professional staff assess student learning through the use of rubrics which include evaluation of students' mastery of information and technology skills as well as content.			

Figure 6.4   Evidence of exemplary collaborative planning

Source: South Carolina Department of Education (2012)

Principals and supervisors can also evaluate the collaborative efforts of the school librarian. The South Carolina Department of Education (2016) has produced guidelines for school library programs performing at an exemplary level. Figure 6.4 is the section on collaborative planning.

Once a curriculum is planned and mapped, individual lessons must be constructed. Harada (2007) provides guidance for designing an integrated lesson plan. It should contain the components shown in figure 6.5 (see page 150).

Evaluation of a Cooperatively Planned Lesson

Reflection on what worked and ways to improve the lesson can be accomplished by having a conversation. To facilitate this conversation, one might want to use the Teacher Evaluation of a Library Lesson or Unit survey (page 148), which provides a starting point for discussions between classroom teachers and the school librarian. A similar survey for obtaining input from students follows the teacher survey.

TEACHER EVALUATION OF A LIBRARY LESSON OR UNIT

Teacher ____ Grade __________

Lesson/Unit ____

Please respond to the following questions using the following scale:

SA = Strongly agree;   A = Agree;   U = Undecided;   D = Disagree;   SD = Strongly Disagree

Students had enough time in the library to achieve the lesson's objectives.	SA	A	U	D	SD
Directions to the assignment were clear.	SA	A	U	D	SD
The library media objectives supported the classroom objectives.	SA	A	U	D	SD
There were enough resources to complete the assignment.	SA	A	U	D	SD
Students were interested in the lesson.	SA	A	U	D	SD
The information presented was at the right level.	SA	A	U	D	SD
Evaluation of the students was appropriate.	SA	A	U	D	SD
I felt comfortable with planning and executing the lesson.	SA	A	U	D	SD

What worked well:

Suggested changes for the next time this lesson is taught:

STUDENT EVALUATION OF A LIBRARY LESSON OR UNIT

Grade __________

Lesson/Unit ____

Please respond to the following questions using the following scale:

SA = Strongly agree;   A = Agree;   U = Undecided;   D = Disagree;   SD = Strongly Disagree

I had enough time in the library to do a good job on this lesson.	SA	A	U	D	SD
Directions to the assignment were clear.	SA	A	U	D	SD
What I did in the library helped me understand this class better.	SA	A	U	D	SD
There were enough resources to complete the assignment.	SA	A	U	D	SD
I was interested in the lesson.	SA	A	U	D	SD
I understood the information presented.	SA	A	U	D	SD
How I was evaluated was fair.	SA	A	U	D	SD

What I liked about this lesson:

What I didn't like about this lesson:

<table>
<tr><th colspan="2" align="center">Lesson Template</th></tr>
<tr><td></td><td align="center">Check when complete</td></tr>
<tr><td colspan="2">Designing the Learning Plan:</td></tr>
<tr><td>1. Title of lesson</td><td></td></tr>
<tr><td>2. Grade level</td><td></td></tr>
<tr><td>3. Content standards addressed (including benchmarks)</td><td></td></tr>
<tr><td>4. Information literacy standards aligned with content standards</td><td></td></tr>
<tr><td>5. Specific learning target for the lesson</td><td></td></tr>
<tr><td>6. Criteria to assess achievement of the learning target</td><td></td></tr>
<tr><td>7. Performance task or object that will be assessed</td><td></td></tr>
<tr><td>8. Tool to use in assessing how well students achieve the learning target</td><td></td></tr>
<tr><td>9. Lesson procedure</td><td></td></tr>
<tr><td>10. Resources for the lesson</td><td></td></tr>
<tr><td colspan="2">During and After Implementation:</td></tr>
<tr><td>11. Assessment results</td><td></td></tr>
<tr><td>12. Reflection on what worked and ways to improve the lesson</td><td></td></tr>
</table>

Figure 6.5   Contents of lesson template

Source: Harada, Violet. 2007. "From Eyeballing to Evidence: Assessing for Learning in Hawaii Library Media Centers." School Library Media Activities Monthly 24 (3): 21-25. ERIC (EJ784568).

STANDARDIZED TESTS

"In many states, teacher evaluation is or will be based, at least partially, on student achievement scores on standardized tests. This approach to evaluation presents a challenge for many school librarians who must provide specific information on which, if any, learning outcomes are taught and measured only in the library" (Moreillon 2013, 24). School librarians have access to test score data, which, when analyzed, can be employed into actionable knowledge to improve student learning and instructional decision making (Marsh, Pane, and Hamilton 2006). For example, if test scores are low for understanding graphs, this skill can be reinforced in elementary school by reading the book *Sir Cumference and the Off-the-Charts Dessert* by Cindy Neuschwander (Winne 2019); in middle school by using the Internet to research "turkey consumption worldwide," graphing the data with a spreadsheet program, analyzing the results, and typing conclusions (TeacherVision 2019); and in high school by using information from the Internet to identify a car and determine the future value of the car using different depreciation rates over different intervals of time. Students will then graph their data to show exponential decay and compare it to a linear decrease on the same graph (Winne 2019). If knowledge and skills are low

Category	Percentile Gain
Identifying similarities and differences	45
Summarizing and note taking	34
Nonlinguistic representations	27
Cooperative learning	27
Setting objectives and providing feedback	23
Questions, cues, and advance organizers	22

Figure 6.6 Instructional strategies that affect student achievement on standardized tests

in areas already being covered in the curriculum, lessons can be changed or reinforced throughout the year.

There are also specific instructional strategies that have been shown to affect student achievement on standardized tests (Marzano, Pickering, and Pollock 2001 as cited in Moreillon 2013). Think about using these strategies shown in figure 6.6 in information literacy instruction.

TEACHER PROFESSIONAL DEVELOPMENT

School librarians are utilized as staff developers because they serve the entire school with a "whole school view" and have an understanding of standards, pedagogy, cultivating learning environments, and curriculum (Abilock, Fontichiaro, and Harada 2012). Staff development can take the form of workshops, mentoring, professional learning communities, coaching, and online communications. Bradburn's (1999) output measures for staff development include the following:

$$\textbf{Staff Development Request Rate} = 100\% \; \frac{\text{\# unmet requests for staff development}}{\text{\# staff development requests received from administrators and teachers}}$$

$$\textbf{Staff Development Attendance Rate} = \frac{\text{\# staff attending sessions}}{\text{\# enrolled staff}}$$

Planning Professional Development

When planning professional development, incorporate the following research findings (Powerful Learning Practice 2015) so that it is valuable to teachers.

Evaluation Level	What Questions Are Addressed?	How Will Information Be Gathered?	What Is Measured or Assessed?	How Will Information Be Used?
1. Participants' Reactions	Did they like it? Was their time well spent? Did the material make sense? Will it be useful? Was the leader knowledgeable and helpful? Were the refreshments fresh and tasty? Was the room the right temperature? Were the chairs comfortable?	Questionnaires administered at the end of the session	Initial satisfaction with the experience	To improve program design and delivery
2. Participants' Learning	Did participants acquire the intended knowledge and skills?	Paper-and-pencil instruments Simulations Demonstrations Participant reflections (oral and/or written) Participant portfolios	New knowledge and skills of participants	To improve program content, format, and organization
3. Organization Support and Change	Was implementation advocated, facilitated, and supported? Was the support public and overt? Were problems addressed quickly and efficiently? Were sufficient resources made available? Were successes recognized and shared? What was the impact on the organization? Did it affect the organization's climate and procedures?	District and school records Minutes from follow-up meetings Questionnaires Structured interviews with participants and district or school administrators Participant portfolios	The organization's advocacy, support, accommodation, facilitation, and recognition	To document and improve organization support To inform future change efforts

Figure 6.7   Five levels of professional development

Source: Guskey, Thomas R. 2002. "Does It Make a Difference? Evaluating Professional Development." *Educational Leadership* 59 (2): 45-51. http://www.ascd.org/publications/educational-leadership/mar02/vol59/num06/Does-It-Make-a-Difference%C2%A2-Evaluating-Professional-Development.aspx.

4. Participants' Use of New Knowledge and Skills	Did participants effectively apply the new knowledge and skills?	Questionnaires Structured interviews with participants and their supervisors Participant reflections (oral and/or written) Participant portfolios Direct observations Video or audio tapes	Degree and quality of implementation	To document and improve the implementation of program content
5. Student Learning Outcomes	What was the impact on students? Did it affect student performance or achievement? Did it influence students' physical or emotional well-being? Are students more confident as learners? Is student attendance improving? Are dropouts decreasing?	Student records School records Questionnaires Structured interviews with students, parents, teachers, and/or administrators Participant portfolios	Student learning outcomes: • Cognitive (Performance & Achievement) • Affective (Attitudes & Dispositions) • Psychomotor (Skills & Behaviors)	To focus and improve all aspects of program design, implementation, and follow-up To demonstrate the overall impact of professional development

Figure 6.7   Continued

Ten Things Teachers Want in Professional Development

1. Teachers want a voice and choice in the professional development offered.
2. Teachers want professional development that is relevant for their students.
3. Teachers want professional development they can use right away.
4. Teachers want professional development that is conducted by professionals with classroom experience.
5. Teachers want professional development that is innovative and creative.
6. Teachers want professional development that makes them better teachers.
7. Teachers want professional development that is practical and not theoretical.
8. Teachers want professional development that allows them to collaborate and speak honestly.
9. Teachers want professional development that will be relevant for a long time.
10. Teachers want administrators to attend and participate in the professional development sessions (Powerful Learning Practice 2015).

Evaluation of Professional Development

Guskey (2002) has constructed a matrix for professional development evaluation based on the collection and analysis of the five critical levels of information shown in figure 6.7. It is recommended that because each level builds on those that come before, success at one level is usually necessary for success at higher levels.

REFERENCES

Abilock, Debbie, Kristin Fontichiaro, and Violet H. Harada, eds. 2012. *Growing Schools: Librarians as Professional Developers.* Santa Barbara, CA: Libraries Unlimited.

Archambault, Susan G., and Jennifer Masunaga. 2015. "Curriculum Mapping as a Strategic Planning Tool." *Journal of Library Administration* 55 (6): 503–519. doi:10.1080/01930826.2015.1054770.

Bradburn, Frances Bryant. 1999. *Output Measures for School Library Media Programs.* New York: Neal-Schuman Publishers.

Danielson Group. 2013. "2013 Framework for Teaching Evaluation Instrument." https://danielsongroup.org/downloads/2013-framework-teaching-evaluation-instrument.

Everhart, Nancy, Marcia Mardis, and Melissa Johnston. 2011. "National Board Certified School Librarians' Leadership in Technology Integration: Results of a National Survey." *School Library Media Research* 14: 1–18. http://www.ala.org/aasl/sites/ala.org.aasl/files/content/aaslpubsand journals/slr/vol14/SLR_NationalBoardCertified_V14.pdf.

Guskey, Thomas R. 2002. "Does It Make a Difference? Evaluating Professional Development." *Educational Leadership* 59 (2): 45–51. http://www.ascd.org/publications/educational-leadership/mar02/vol59/num06/Does-It-Make-a-Difference%C2%A2-Evaluating-Professional-Development.aspx.

Harada, Violet. 2007. "From Eyeballing to Evidence: Assessing for Learning in Hawaii Library Media Centers." *School Library Media Activities Monthly* 24 (3): 21–25. ERIC (EJ784568).

Loertscher, David V. 2000. *Taxonomies of the School Library Media Program.* 2nd ed. San Jose, CA: Hi Willow Research & Pub.

Marsh, Julie A., John F. Pane, and Laura S. Hamilton. 2006. "Making Sense of Data-Driven Decision Making in Education: Evidence from Recent RAND Research." Santa Monica, CA: RAND Corporation. https://www.rand.org/pubs/occasional_papers/OP170.html.

Merga, Margaret Kristin. 2019. "Do Librarians Feel That Their Profession Is Valued in Contemporary Schools?" *Journal of the Australian Library and Information Association* 68 (1): 18–37. doi:10.1080/24750158.2018.1557979.

Moreillon, Judi. 2013. "Educating for School Library Leadership: Developing the Instructional Partnership Role." *Journal of Education for Library and Information Science* 54 (1): 55–66. ERIC (EJ1074121).

Powerful Learning Practice. 2015. "10 Things Teachers Want in Professional Development." Last modified August 28. https://plpnetwork.com/2015/08/28/10-teachers-professional-development.

Sherrington, Tom. 2019. "How Well Do You Know Your School's Curriculum?" Schools Week, Last modified March 3. https://schoolsweek.co.uk/how-well-do-you-know-your-schools-curriculum.

South Carolina Department of Education. 2016. "South Carolina Standards for School Library Resource Collections." https://ed.sc.gov/educators/school-and-district-administrators/certified-support-specialists/library-media-specialists/standards-for-school-library-resource-collections.

TeacherVision. 2019. "Graphing Turkey Consumption." https://www.teacher vision.com/spreadsheet-skills/graphing-turkey-consumption.

Weisburg, Hilda K., and Ruth Toor. 2015. *New on the Job: A School Librarian's Guide to Success*. 2nd ed. Chicago: ALA Editions.

Winne, Brenda. 2019. "Graphing Fun." CPALMS. https://www.cpalms .org/Public/PreviewResourceLesson/Preview/73088.

Chapter 7

Community

The National Board for Professional Teaching Standards (2012) strongly recommends that specialists (school librarians):

> seek out and participate in opportunities to generate enthusiasm for library media programs among families and other members of the greater community. Specialists enlist the aid of families, volunteers, and other partners by using frequent communications to encourage input. Specialists provide the learning community with opportunities to evaluate the program's effectiveness and to make suggestions to help determine the library program's direction. For example, as a result of community input, accomplished library media specialists may reach out to families of English language learners by crafting a specific library orientation program that highlights available resources.
>
> With the goals of strengthening library media programs and expanding multiple literacies, specialists welcome partnerships with educational and cultural institutions, such as public libraries, university libraries, community agencies, and museums. Specialists may offer open houses, online communications, and school and community presentations to develop awareness and promote learning. Specialists promote the core values of the profession, such as intellectual freedom and access to information, to the school community and beyond. They offer evidence-based reporting to inform

community stakeholders about the library media program and its achievements. (49)

Research has shown that school librarians express anxiety about how to demonstrate involvement in the local communities (Everhart, Mardis, and Johnston 2011). Yet, reaching out to community stakeholders in an organized, purposeful way can garner substantial support for school libraries and school librarians (Mardis and Everhart 2014).

The Texas state standards and guidelines for school library programs is one of very few that offers specific examples for community involvement in their rubric (Texas State Library and Archives Commission and the Texas Education Agency 2017).

KNOWLEDGE OF THE COMMUNITY

To engage with the local community, knowledge of that community is required. There are sources of data which you can use to become more familiar with your community. Similar to the checklist found in chapter 6 on knowledge of the school, the one in table 7.1 can be employed to determine the level of knowledge of the school's external community.

Types of Engagement

Various forms of community engagement have been discussed by school librarians in the Facebook group Future Ready Librarians (2019). Shown in table 7.2, these provide ideas on where you might start.

Table 7-1   Knowledge of School's External Community

	Aware	Unaware	Need Info	Source
Households (size, ethnicities, ages, income, educational attainment)				factfinder.census.gov
Population density				factfinder.census.gov
Transient rate				factfinder.census.gov
Poverty level				factfinder.census.gov
Businesses, major employers				factfinder.census.gov
Crime rate				city-data.com/crime
Home value				Zillow.com
Broadband (deployment, providers)				broadbandmap.fcc.gov/#

Table 7-2   Types of Community Engagement

Check the appropriate box

Yes	No	Consider	
☐	☐	☐	Guest readers
☐	☐	☐	Career fair with guest speakers
☐	☐	☐	Adult/child book club
☐	☐	☐	Book fair open to the public
☐	☐	☐	Read-to-me program with local preschools
☐	☐	☐	Coordinated events with local bookstore, such as author visits
☐	☐	☐	Little Free Library
☐	☐	☐	Therapy dogs
☐	☐	☐	Public library cooperation
☐	☐	☐	Volunteers (parents or community members)
☐	☐	☐	Museum partnerships
☐	☐	☐	Friends of the Library group
☐	☐	☐	Use digital resources to produce a book/video about the community.
☐	☐	☐	Artist/writer in residence
☐	☐	☐	PTO/parent club
☐	☐	☐	Library column in school newsletter or town newspaper
☐	☐	☐	Advisory committee
☐	☐	☐	Community open house/celebration
☐	☐	☐	Family literacy night
☐	☐	☐	Prepare an elevator speech for when you interact with the public and they ask about your position.

Communicating with the Public

Barber and Wallace (2010) suggest conducting a communication audit to examine the many ways the public library is communicating with the public. These questions can be used or adapted for school libraries.

1. *Accessibility*—Can people easily navigate the library building and website?
2. *Brand/Identity*—Does the library have a clear, consistent image?
3. *Customer service*—Is the library staff committed to excellent customer service?
4. *Listening*—Do staff members listen and act on feedback?
5. *Decor/Decoration*—Is the library well lit, uncluttered, and attractively decorated?

6. *Display*—Are the books displayed effectively?
7. *Local ownership*—Does the library reflect the diversity of the community and act on its behalf?
8. *Message*—Does the library have a message that is effectively communicated?
9. *Media*—Does the library have a media presence?
10. *Outreach*—Does the library have a presence in the community outside the library building?
11. *Programming*—Does the library actively offer and promote programming?
12. *Print materials*—Are there an effective number of clear, attractive print materials containing the library's message?
13. *Signage*—Is the library easy to find?
14. *Telephone*—Does someone answer the phone and act on calls?
15. *Website*—Is the website message consistent with other library communications?
16. *Body language*—What is the unspoken message being delivered by staff?

CONSISTENT MESSAGING

In 2010–2011, I visited thirty-six outstanding school libraries throughout the United States on what I called a "Vision Tour" to highlight great programs to the general community (Everhart 2013). I had a logo created and even a theme song that was composed by a music student. Consistent messaging is effective in outreach.

One component of consistent messaging is to devise a slogan or tagline. The American Library Association has created taglines such as Libraries Transform and @Your Library with accompanying promotional materials. Myriad slogans can be found on Pinterest using the search term "library slogans." According to Lamb (2019), slogans, or taglines, for school libraries can be evaluated using the following criteria:

- Is the tagline easy to remember?
- Does the tagline reflect the mission?
- Does the tagline emote a positive emotional feeling?
- Does the tagline feel comfortable and natural?
- Does the tagline reflect the character of the library?
- Does the tagline set the library apart from other libraries and organizations?

Logos are used in businesses to distinguish them from the competition. School libraries can also have logos that will identify them and project their value. Effective logos have the following characteristics:

- *Memorable*—A logo should be distinct or unique in some way.
- *Simple*—Simple shapes and color combinations make logos easy to recognize.
- *Timeless*—Trendy styles and typefaces might look great today, but how will they look in five to ten years?
- *Appropriate*—The overall style, colors, and typefaces should speak to the audience of the logo or organization.
- *Versatile*—A good logo adapts to different colors, sizes, and mediums (imagine how it will look on a business card, website, T-shirt, or billboard) (Hall 2015).

DIGITAL ANALYTICS

One approach to engage with the community is through digital and social media. Does your library have a website, Facebook, Instagram, or Twitter account? Each of these platforms have free analytical tools to track user engagement with your content. You can also monitor them simultaneously with a fee-based application such as Hootsuite. It is recommended that the following data points be collected:

- *Audience*—The number of followers/subscribers and their demographic data when possible. This basic user data shows who is looking at or listening to your social media content.
- *Engagement*—The number of views, likes, or comments a social media post or content receives. This can include multiple data points, depending on your social media platform, but all describe how much attention your social media account received.
- *Sharing*—The number of shares or reposting of your library's content by social media users. This is a super-engagement metric, as it shows users interacting with your social media content and sending it to their followers.
- *Sentiment*—A subset of sharing metrics focusing on how social media users describe your content or organization. Sharing content can be a good or bad thing depending on how users describe or relate to the content they repost.

- *Referral*—Traffic generated from social media to another website, such as the library's main site.
- *Conversions*—Desired actions performed by your social media users, such as when users are directed to your online presence. (Farney 2018, 24)

Data Visualization

Data visualization is defined by Google Dictionary as "the representation of information in the form of a chart, diagram, picture, etc." It is used to make complex data more accessible, understandable, and usable.

Infographics

Infographics, or information graphics, are one form of data visualization. They are useful for synthesizing and displaying large amounts of information, making it understandable and visually appealing (Creighton 2015). For example, school librarians make use of infographics to create monthly or annual reports as shown in figure 7.1

The Library Research Service in Colorado produces infographics (summary and expanded versions) for every school that responds to the Colorado School Library Survey (lrs.org/data-tools/school-libraries/school-library-profiles). Profiles for each participating school compare individual school data with averages for schools with similar grade level and enrollment ranges (Library Research Service 2019).

Library Dashboards

Like infographics, library dashboards are visual tools that offer insights into a library's operations at one glance. They get their name from car dashboards, where you can see how your car is performing in a second or two (Huber and Potter 2015). Dashboards differ from infographics in that they are fluid rather than static.

> There are two primary goals for dashboards: marketing and success. One seeks to advertise the excellence of the library—perhaps to secure further funding, perhaps to raise its profile on campus—while the other aims at improved daily operations, however that may be defined. These are two terrifically broad categories, but they create a useful distinction when building a dashboard. (Phetteplace 2014)

It is recommended that community pyramid dashboard metrics meet the following criteria:

- Easy to collect and analyze
- Proactive rather than reactive

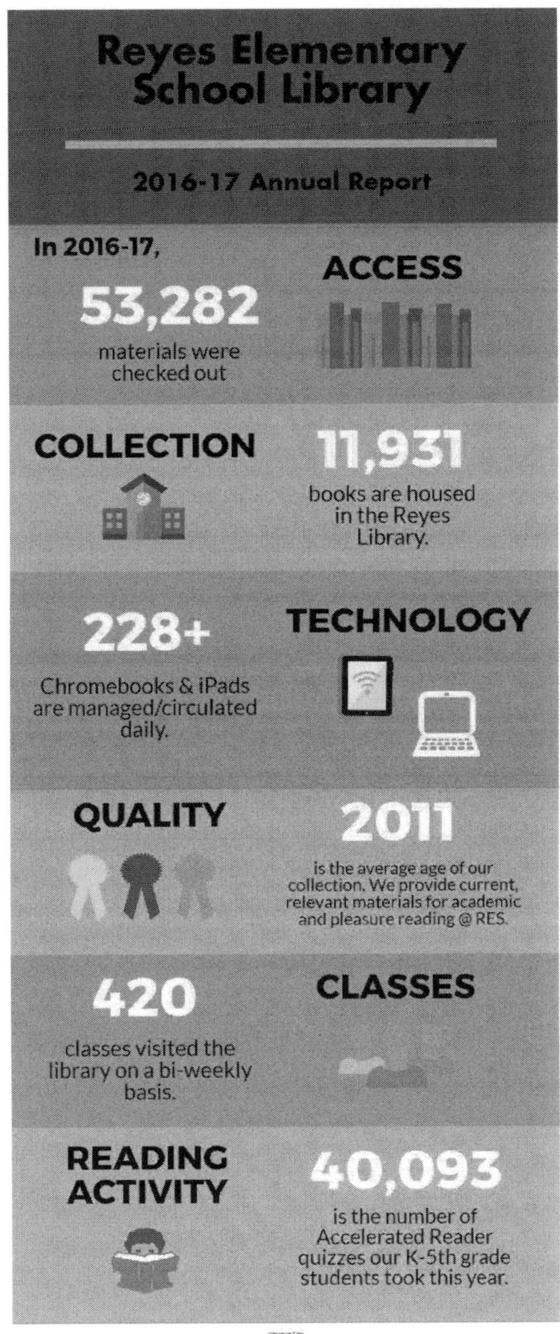

Figure 7.1   Annual report in infographic form

Source: Reprinted with permission of Julie Hoy.

- Visual
- Simple and easily understood
- Show a causal relationship
- Provide a value perspective of the improvements
- Driven in both a top-down and bottom-up direction (Huber and Potter 2015)

There are many data sources available, but selecting those metrics that will promote a positive image of the library program is essential. You may want to refer back to some of the output measures throughout this book, such as average visits per student, average book checkouts per student, attendance per month (day or year), a list of projects this week (month), special events, databases by popularity, online visits, and average daily searches, among others. Graphics from an infographic can be incorporated. The metrics that are ultimately chosen should relate to your objectives for the dashboard. The data can be visualized by using simple tools, such as Google Data Studio, Google Charts, or Excel. Many school libraries use the Destiny management system, which has a dashboard reporting option. Academic and public libraries that provide dashboards use Tableau to organize and display large amounts of data.

Few examples of school library dashboards exist in the literature; however, one exception is Hommocks Middle School in Larchmont, New York, where school librarian Kelsey Cohen (2018) displays reading choices: number of books read by Hommocks students this year, most read this month (by title), types of books, and books per grade. Cohen displays these colorful graphics on a large monitor in the library, but they could easily be displayed on a large monitor in the school lobby or on the library or school website.

PARENTS

Parents can provide useful feedback about the school library program. By administering an anonymous survey, you can find out what they support and what areas are of concern (see Parent Survey, page 165). The mere act of soliciting parents' opinions will make them feel involved and may also garner other good ideas and suggestions.

PLANNING A CELEBRATION

It is important to get the community into the school library, and one method for doing so is to plan some sort of celebratory event. During my aforementioned Vision Tour, I had asked each school librarian to plan an event and invite a local celebrity and decision makers along with anyone else who wanted to come. One thing the Vision Tour did was to get many decision makers into school libraries. These rallies, receptions, programs, and assemblies that were dedicated to celebrating a school library program gave the school librarians a good reason to invite people in. I heard over and over again, "This is the first time my superintendent has been in my library." A number of annual events can serve as a reason: National School Library Month and National Library Week, Read Across America Day, Teen Read Week, and Children's Book Week. Invite those who are key to supporting your school library program and give them something to do: read a poem,

PARENT SURVEY

1. Are you familiar with your school library and the services it provides?
    ________ Yes   ________ No

2. If your answer to question 1 was "yes," how would you rate the service of the library?
    _______ Excellent   _______ Good   _______ Fair   _______ Poor

3. Does your child use the facilities of the school library?
    _______ Frequently   _______ Occasionally   _______ Never   _______ Don't know

4. Are library materials sufficient for your child's needs?
    _______ Yes   _______ No   _______ Don't know

5. Does your child have access to the library and school librarian throughout the school day?
    _______ Yes   _______ No   _______ Don't know

6. Do you feel your child finds it necessary to use other libraries in the community to complete assignments?
    _______ Yes   _______ No   _______ Don't know

7. Do your child's teachers use and encourage student use of library resources?
    _______ Yes   _______ No   _______ Don't know

8. Do your child's research projects use a variety of technologies to locate and use information?
    _______ Yes   _______ No   _______ Don't know

9. Have you visited your child's library?
    _______ Yes   _______ No

10. Have you accessed the library's website?
    _______ Yes   _______ No

11. What suggestions do you have to make the library program better?

make a speech, present an award, or introduce others. The School Preparation Checklist (page 167) contains components that I used for the Vision Tour for school librarians to plan an event.

EVALUATING OUTREACH

Outreach is a way for school libraries to promote their services, demonstrate value by engaging with stakeholders, and show their usefulness and relevance in today's modern world (Farrell and Mastel 2016; Graves, LeMire, Mastel, and Farrell 2018). Planning and conducting outreach events is time-consuming. Using metrics to assess outreach programming will enable you to demonstrate their impact and the library's value (table 7.3). Measure the success of these events with outcomes in mind—what you want participants to know or be able to do. For example, one outreach outcome could be that during a technology open house, participants will learn at least one new technology skill. The desired measurable outcomes will determine the evaluation strategy and the data collected.

Using the aforementioned outcome, assessment might look something like that in table 7.4.

After an outreach event, simple reflection may divulge areas that can be improved upon for the future. The assessment data can also be used to compile a report or presentation for administrators to demonstrate the library's value.

SCHOOL PREPARATION CHECKLIST

1. **School library recognition event**

    a.   What groups do you expect to attend?

    b.   How many people do you expect to attend?

    c.   What do you have planned for the event (e.g., pep rally, press conference, small event in the library, etc.)? Please explain in detail or attach an agenda.

    d.   When will the event take place (time of day)?

    e.   Where will the event be held?

    f.   If this is for a large crowd, will you have a sound system set up?

    g.   Will you be using music? If so, in what context?

    h.   Plan to give a ten-minute speech at this event. Be prepared to speak extemporaneously without PowerPoint slides.

2. **Photography**

    a.   Who will take photographs and video footage?

3. **Publicity**

    a.   Who from the press was contacted about the event?

    b.   Who from the press do you expect to be at the event?

    c.   Have you invited a local celebrity or dignitary?

    d.   Press

        i.   Prepare press releases.

        ii.   Keep copies of any press coverage—newspapers, TV, radio.

4. **Food**

    a.   Will you serve refreshments?

    b.   Did you appoint a refreshments committee?

    c.   Will refreshments be donated or purchased? Where will funds come from?

Table 7-3 Outreach Assessment Strategies

Strategy	Description	Quantitative or Qualitative?	Considerations and Limitations
Capturing comments	Collect thoughts of motivated participants on paper, whiteboards, or other media.	Qualitative	They are easy to capture, but responses can be influenced by other comments that are visible; people with differing opinions may not participate.
Compiling social media comments or press cuttings	Gather coverage of an event through social media, newspapers, and other media outlets.	Qualitative	Not all attendees are active on social media, and attendees might use different platforms or hashtags from those used by the event organizers.
Documentation	Capture photographs and anecdotes in a document or report to paint an overall picture of an event.	Qualitative	May require release forms, and not all participants will want to participate; the approach also gathers only a snapshot of one or more points in time.
Focus groups	Interview participants in groups after the event.	Both	This is time-intensive for staff and participants; it may require monetary (or other) reward for participating as well as extensive coding afterward.
Head counts	Count the number of people present at an event.	Quantitative	This is quick and easy, but it does not address engagement or why people attend
Mini interviews during the event	Conduct brief interviews during the event.	Both	Some staff time is needed, and it may also require coding, depending on the questions; not all participants will be comfortable in an interview, so a confident interviewer is needed to elicit interesting responses.
Minute papers	Ask participants to take one minute to write down an answer to a question.	Qualitative	Overall, this is quick and easy, but it may not elicit reflective/thoughtful responses; it will require some coding afterward.

Continued

Table 7-3   Continued

Strategy	Description	Quantitative or Qualitative?	Considerations and Limitations
Mystery shoppers	Recruit trained undercover volunteers to evaluate your event and report their experiences.	Both	It could be a challenge to recruit "shoppers" who are unfamiliar to staff, and it requires a fair amount of time to create an evaluation form and code the responses.
Observations during the event	Note how participants move through the event and how they interface and interact with the event's content.	Both	Participants' activities and motivations may be misinterpreted.
Surveys	Administer questionnaires to participants at or following the event.	Both	Time is required to come up with good questions and code the responses.
Vox pops	Document participants' thoughts and feelings via short audio or video recordings.	Qualitative	Requires staff familiar with equipment and technology; many attendees may not be comfortable being on camera.

Source: Graves, LeMire, Mastel, and Farrell (2018)

Table 7-4   Example Outreach Activity

Outcome	Assessment		Activity
Technology open house attendees will learn at least one new technology skill.	Capturing comments	A graffiti wall with the prompt "What new tech skill did you learn today?"	Learning stations set up throughout the library
	Vox pops using a video discussion platform	Short interviews with selected participants about what most surprised them about tech services in the library	
	Survey	An electronic follow-up survey sent to those who left their e-mail address	

Source: Adapted from Table 3. Graves, LeMire, Mastel, and Farrell (2018)

REFERENCES

Barber, Peggy, and Linda Wallace. 2010. *Building a Buzz: Libraries & Word-of-Mouth Marketing*. Chicago: American Library Association.

Cohen, Kelsey. 2018. "Supporting Middle School Reading: Using a Data Dashboard to Create a Community of Readers." *American Libraries*, June 1. https://americanlibrariesmagazine.org/2018/06/01/supporting-middle -school-reading.

Creighton, Peggy Milam. 2015. *School Library Infographics: How to Create Them, Why to Use Them*. Santa Barbara, CA: Libraries Unlimited.

Everhart, Nancy. 2013. "Defining a Vision of Outstanding School Libraries." *Teacher Librarian* 41 (1): 14–16. EBSCOhost (91262433).

Everhart, Nancy, Marcia Mardis, and Melissa Johnston. 2011. "National Board Certified School Librarians' Leadership in Technology Integration: Results of a National Survey." *School Library Media Research* 14: 1–18. http://www.ala.org/aasl/sites/ala.org.aasl/files/content/aaslpubsand journals/slr/vol14/SLR_NationalBoardCertified_V14.pdf.

Farney, Tabatha. 2018. *Using Digital Analytics for Smart Assessment*. Chicago: ALA Editions.

Farrell, Shannon L., and Kristen Mastel. 2016. "Considering Outreach Assessment: Strategies, Sample Scenarios, and a Call to Action." *In the Library with the Lead Pipe*, May 4. http://www.inthelibrarywiththe leadpipe.org/2016/considering-outreach-assessment-strategies-sample -scenarios-and-a-call-to-action/.

Future Ready Librarians. 2019. "Future Ready Librarians' Facebook Page." August 22, 2019. https://www.facebook.com/groups/futureready librarians.

Graves, Stephine, Sarah LeMire, Kristen Mastel, and Shannon Farrell. 2018. "Demonstrating Library Value through Outreach Goals and Assessment." EDUCAUSE Review, August 13. https://er.educause .edu/articles/2018/8/demonstrating-library-value-through-outreach-goals -and-assessment.

Hall, Sheri. 2015. "How to Design an Infographic." Soleil Design. http:// soleildesign.com/wordpress/wp-content/uploads/soleildesign-diy-logo -design-fnl.pdf.

Huber, John J., and Steven V. Potter. 2015. *The Purpose-Based Library: Finding Your Path to Survival, Success, and Growth*. Chicago: Neal-Schuman.

Lamb, Annette. 2019. "Message Design, Branding & the Library's Story." *Marketing for Libraries* (blog), *EDUSCAPES*. https://iu.app.box.com/s/ayw8vth0huaqx50ltrkid6l6a3d50xtc.

Library Research Service. 2019. "Colorado School Library Profiles." https://www.lrs.org/data-tools/school-libraries/school-library-profiles.

Mardis, Marcia A., and Nancy Everhart. 2014. "Stakeholders as Researchers: A Multiple Case Study of Using Cooperative Inquiry to Develop and Document the Formative Leadership Experiences of New School Library Professionals." *Library and Information Science Research* 36 (1): 3–15. doi:10.1016/j.lisr.2013.08.002.

National Board for Professional Teaching Standards. 2012. *Library Media Standards*. http://accomplishedteacher.org/wp-content/uploads/2017/02/ECYA-LM.pdf.

Phetteplace, Eric. 2014. "Building a Data Dashboard." *ACRL TechConnect* (blog), American Library Association, November 12. https://acrl.ala.org/techconnect/post/building-a-data-dashboard/.

Texas State Library and Archives Commission and the Texas Education Agency. 2017. *School Library Programs: Standards and Guidelines for Texas*. https://www.tsl.texas.gov/sites/default/files/public/tslac/ld/school libs/sls/Texas%20School%20Library%20Standards%20E-Version%20FINAL.pdf.

INDEX

ABOUT THE AUTHOR

DR. NANCY EVERHART is a professor at the iSchool at Florida State University. She is an award-winning researcher and the author of over one hundred professional articles focusing on school librarians and school libraries. She serves as coeditor of *School Libraries Worldwide* and is a former president of the American Association of School Librarians and a Fulbright Scholar.